Narrative
of the Captivity of
William Biggs

Among the Kickapoo Indians
in Illinois in 1788

&

Narrative
of the Captivity
and Restoration of
Mrs. Mary Rowlandson

Printed on acid free ANSI archival quality paper.
ISBN: 978-1-78139-095-5
© 2012 Benediction Classics, Oxford.

Contents

Narrative of the Captivity of William Biggs

Among the Kickapoo Indians in Illinois in 1788

Narrative of
William Biggs

In the year 1788, March 28th, I was going from Bellfontain
to Cahokia, in company with a young man named John Vallis,
from the State of Maryland; he was born and raised near Balti-
more. About 7 o'clock in the morning I heard two guns fired; by
the report I thought they were to the right; I thought they were
white men hunting; both shot at the same time. I looked but
could not see any body; in a moment after I looked to the left
and saw sixteen Indians, all upon their feet with their guns presented, about forty yards distant from me, just ready to draw
trigger. I was riding between Vallis and the Indians in a slow
trot, at the moment I saw them. I whipped my horse and leaned
my breast on the horse's withers, and told Vallis to whip his
horse, that they were Indians. That moment they all fired their
guns in one platoon; you could scarcely distinguish the report of
their guns one from another. They shot four bullets into my
horse, one high up in his withers, one in the bulge of the ribs
near my thigh, and two in his rump, and shot four or five
through my great coat. The moment they fired their guns they
ran towards us and yelled so frightfully, that the wounds and
the yelling of the Indians scared my horse so that he jumped so
suddenly to one side of the road, that my gun fell off my shoul-

der, and twisted out of my hand; I then bore all my weight on one stirrup, in order to catch my gun, but could not. I had a large bag of beaver fur, which prevented me from recovering my saddle, and having no girth nor crupper to my saddle, it turned and fell off my horse, and I fell with it, but caught on my feet and held the mane; I made several attempts to mount my horse again; but the Indians running up so close, and making such a frightful yelling, that my horse jumped and pranced so that it was impossible for me to mount him again, but I held fast to my horse's mane for twenty or thirty yards; then my hold broke and I fell on my hands and knees, and stumbled along about four or five steps before I could recover myself. By the time I got fairly on my feet, the Indians were about eight or ten yards from me— I saw then there was no other way for me to make my escape but by fast running, and I was determined to try it, and had but little hopes at first of my being able to escape. I ran about one hundred yards before I looked back—I thought almost every step I could feel the scalping knife cutting my scalp off. I found I was gaining ground on them, I felt encouraged and ran about three hundred yards farther, and looking back saw that I had gained about one hundred yards, and considering myself quite out of danger. A thought then occurred to me, that I was as safe and out of danger as I would be if I were in the City of Philadelphia: the Indians had quit yelling and slacked their running—but I did not know it then. It being a tolerable cold morning and I was heavily clad, I thought perhaps the Indians would give me a long chase, and probably that they would hold out better than I could; although at that time I did not feel the least tired or out of breath. I concluded to throw off my two coats and shoes, as I would then be better prepared for a long race. I had my great coat tied around me with a silk handkerchief pretty much worn—I recollect tying it with a slip knot, but being in a hurry, it was drawn into a double hard knot; I tried some little time to get it loose—the longer I tried the harder the knot seemed to get, that stopped my running considerably; at length I broke it by some means, I do not know how. In the morning I forgot to put on my shot pouch before I put on my great coat, and then put it on over it. I pulled off the sleeves of my great coat, not thinking of my shot-pouch being over my coat, it having a very short strap, the coat got so tight in the strap that I could not get it loose for a considerable time. Still trying, it hung down and trailed on the ground, and every two or three steps it would wrap around my legs and throw me down, and I would catch on my hands and knees, it served me so several times, so that I could make no headway at running. After some considerable time, I broke the strap and my great coat dropped from me—I had no knife with me.

The Indians discovered that something was the matter and saw me tumbling down several times. I suppose they thought I was wounded and could run no farther; they then set up the yell again and mended their gait running. By the time I got my great coat loose from me, and was in the act of pulling off my under coat, I was pulling off one sleeve I looked back over my shoulder, but had not time to pull it off—the Indians being within ten yards of me. I then started again to run, but could not gain any ground on them, nor they on me; we ran about one hundred yards farther and neither appeared to gain ground: there was a small pathway that was a little nearer than to keep the big road,—I kept the big road, the Indians took the path, and when we came where the path comes into the big road the Indians were within three or four yards from me—we ran forty or fifty steps farther and neither appeared to gain ground. I expected every moment they would strike me with their tomahawks—I thought it would not do to be killed running like a coward and saw no other way to make my escape than to face about and to catch the tomahawk from the first that attempted to strike me, and jerk it from him, which I made no doubt but I was able to do; then I would have a weapon to fight with as well as them, and by that means I would be able to make my escape; they had thrown down their guns before they gave me chase, but I had not fairly faced about before an Indian caught me by the shoulder and held his tomahawk behind him and made no attempt to strike me. I then thought it best for me not to make any resistance till I would see whether he would attempt to strike me or not. He held me by the shoulder till another came up and took hold of me, which was only four or five moments; then a third

Indian came up, the first Indian that took hold of me took the handle of his tomahawk and rubbed it on my shoulder and down my arm, which was a token that he would not kill me and that I was his prisoner. Then they all took their hands off me and stood around me. The fourth Indian came up and attempted to strike me, but the first Indian that caught me pushed him away. He was still determined to kill me, and tried to get around to my back; but I still faced round as he was trying to get to my back—when he got up by my side, he drew his tomahawk the second time to strike me, but the same Indian pushed him off and scolded him very much—he let his tomahawk hang by his side, but still intended to kill me if he could get an opportunity. The other Indians watched him very closely. There were but four Indians that gave me chase, they were all naked except their breachcloth, leggins and moccasins. They then began to talk to me in their own language, and said they were Kickapoos, that they were very good Indians, and I need not be afraid, they would not hurt me, and I was now a Kickapoo and must go with them, they would take me to the Matocush, meaning a French trading town on the Wabash river. When the Indians caught me I saw Mr. Vallis about one hundred yards before me on the road—he had made a halt. They shot him in the left thigh about seven or eight inches above the knee, the ball came out just below his hip, his horse was not injured—he rode an elegant horse which carried him out of all farther danger—his wound mortified, he lived six weeks after he was wounded, then died. I understood their language, and could speak a little. They then told me to march; an Indian took hold of each of my arms, and led me back to where they shot at me, and then went about half a mile further off the road, where they had encamped the night before and left their blankets and other things. They then took off my under coat and tied my hands behind my back, and then tied a rope to that, tying about six or seven feet long, we then started in a great hurry, and an Indian held one end of the rope while we were marching. There were but eight Indians marched in company with me that morning from the camp. The other eight took some other route, and never fell in with us again, until some time after we got to their towns. We had marched

6

about three or four miles from that camp when Vallis arrived at the fort, about six miles from where they caught me, where they fired a swivel to alarm the people who were out of the fort—when the Indians heard the swivel they were very much alarmed, and all looked that way and hallowed yough, yough. They then commenced running, and run in a pretty smart trot of a run for five or six miles before they halted, and then walked very fast until about 2 o'clock in the afternoon, when they separated, I supposed to hunt, having nothing to eat. The old chief and one of the other Indians kept on a straight course with me, we traveled about three miles, when we got a little way into a small prairie and halted about fifteen minutes, there one of the party fell in with us, he had killed a bear and brought as much of the meat with him as he could carry. We then crossed the prairie and came to a large run about one mile and a half from where we had halted to rest. By this time three Indians had joined us. We halted there, made a fire and roasted the bear meat, the other two Indians staid behind as spies. Whilst the meat was cooking, the Indians held a council what they would do with the Indian that wanted to kill me. He was a young fellow about 19 years of age and of a different nation, being a Pottowatema. They did not want him to go to war with them; they said he was a great coward and would not go into danger till there was no risk to run, then he would run forward and get the best of the plunder, and that he would not be commanded; he would do as he pleased; was very selfish and stubborn; and was determined to kill me if he could get a chance. They determined in their council to kill him. It is a law with the Indians when they go to war, if an Indian will not obey the counsels and commands of his captain or chief, to kill them. When their meat was cooked, they ate very hearty, and when they were done eating, three of the Indians got up, put on their budgets and started, this young Indian was one of them. I also got up to show a willingness to be ready. The old chief told me to sit down, and the three Indians started off. In about three or four minutes after we started, but varied a little in our course. We had not traveled more than one hundred yards when we heard the report of a gun. The old chief then told me that they had killed the Indian that wanted to kill me. The

7

other two Indians fell in company with us before night. We then traveled till about 10 o'clock in the night, when we encamped at a large grove of timber in a prairie, about four miles from the edge of the woods; made no fire that night. We traveled about forty miles that day. After they rested a while they sat down to eat their jirk. They gave me some but I could not eat any. After they were done eating, one of the Indians was sitting with his back against a tree, with his knife between his legs. I was sitting facing him with my feet nearly touching his. He began to inquire of me of what nation I belonged to. I was determined to pretend that I was ignorant and could not understand him. I did not wish them to know that I could speak some Indian language, and understand them better than I could speak. He first asked me in Indian if I was a Matocush, (that is a Frenchman in English). I told him no. He asked me if I was a Sagenash, (an Englishman). I told him no. He again asked if I was a Shemolsea, (that is a long knife or a Virginian). I told him no. He then asked me if I was a Bostonely, (that is American). I told him no. About one minute afterwards, he asked me the same questions over again. I then answered him yes; he then spoke English and caught up his knife in his hand, and said "you are one dam son of a bitch." I really thought he intended stabbing me with his knife. I knew it would not do to show cowardice, I being pretty well acquainted with their manner and ways. I then jumped upon my feet and spoke in Indian and said manetway, kien, depaway, in English it is no, I am very good, and clapped my hand on my breast when I spoke and looked very bold; the other Indians all set up such ha! ha! and laugh that it made the other Indian look very foolish. He sat still and looked very sulky. After they had rested a while, they began to prepare to lay down. They spread down a deer-skin and blanket for me to lay on. They had tied a rope around my arms above my elbows, and tied that rope across my back, and a rope around my neck; they then tied the end of another rope behind to the neck rope, then down my back to the pinion rope; then they drew my hands forward across my stomach and crossed my wrists; then tied my wrists very tight; then tied my legs together, just below my knees; then tied my feet together with a rope round my ankles; then took a

8

small cord and tied in between my wrists, and also between my ankles very tight, in order to prevent me from drawing out my hands or feet; they then took another cord and tied one end to the neck rope; then to the hand rope; then from the hand rope to the knee rope; they then took a rope about six feet long and tied one end to the wrist rope, and the other end to a stake about six feet from me stretched very tight, and an Indian laid on that rope all night; then they took another rope about the same length, and tied one end to the knee rope and the other end to a stake, and another Indian laid on that all night; then they tied a large half-dressed elk rope, one end to the back part of the neck rope which made a knot as big as my fist, the other end they tied to a stake about six feet from my head. When they finished their tying me, they covered me with a blanket. They tied me in the aforegoing way nine nights in succession; they had me stretched and tied so tight, that I could not move one inch to turn or rest myself; that large knot was on the back of my neck, so that I was obliged to lay on it all night, and it hurt my neck very much. I never suffered as much in the same length of time in all my life; I could hardly walk when we got out to their town. They never made me carry anything except a blanket they gave me to keep myself warm, when they took all my clothes from me. The Indians carried a deer-skin and blanket all the way for me to lodge upon. When my hands and feet became sore with the tying the Indians would always pull off my moccasins at night and put them on in the morning, and patch them when they would require it.

The second day we started very early in the morning and traveled about thirty-five miles, which was the 29th of March.

The third day we traveled about thirty miles, which was the 30th of March. They killed a deer that day—in the evening they took the intestines out of the deer and freed them of their contents, when they put them in the kettles with some meat and made soup, I could not eat any of it.

The fourth day we traveled about twenty-five miles. We stopped about 3 o'clock in the afternoon at a pond. They staid there all night. They had some dried meat, tallow, and buffalo marrow, rendered up together, lashed and hung upon a tree about twenty feet from the ground, which they had left there in order to be sure to have something to eat on their return. They killed two ducks that evening. The ducks were very fat. They picked one of the ducks, and took out all its entrils very nice and clean, then stuck it on a stick, and stuck the other end of the stick in the ground before the fire, and roasted it very nice. By the time the duck was cooked, one of the Indians went and cut a large block out of a tree to lay the duck upon; they made a little hole in the ground to catch the fat of the duck while roasting. When the duck was cooked, they laid it on this clean block of wood, then took a spoon and tin cup, and lifted the grease of the duck out of the hole and took it to the cooked duck on the table, and gave me some salt, then told me to go and eat. I sat by and eat the whole of the duck, and could have eat more if I would have had anything more to eat, though I had no bread. I thought I had never eat anything before that tasted so good. That was the first meal I had eaten for four days. The other duck they pulled a few of the largest feathers out off, then threw the duck, guts, feathers and all into their soup-kettle, and cooked it in that manner.

The fifth day we traveled about thirty miles. That night I felt very tired and sore, my hands, arms, legs and feet had swelled and inflamed very much, by this time; the tying that night hurt me very much, I thought I could not live until morning; it felt just like a rough saw cutting my bones. I told the Indians I could not bear it, it would kill me before morning, and asked them to unslack or unloose the wrist rope a little, that hurt me the most. They did so, and rather more than I expected, so much that I could draw my hands out of the tying, which I intended to do as soon as I thought the Indians were asleep. When I thought the Indians were all asleep I drew my right hand out of tying, with an intention to put it back again before I would go to sleep, for fear I should make some stir in my sleep and they might discover me. But, finding so much more ease, and resting so much better, I fell asleep before I knew it, without putting my hand back into the tying. The first thing I knew about 3 o'clock in the morning, an Indian was sitting astraddle me, drawing his tomahawk and rubbing it across my forehead, every time he would draw a stroke with the pipe of his tomahawk, he threatened to kill me, and saying I wanted to run away; I told him to kill away. I would as leave die as live. I then told him I was not able to run away. He then got off me, and the rest of the Indians were all up immediately. They then held a short council and agreed to tie me as tight as ever, and they did so. I got no more sleep that night. I never asked them to loose my ropes any more.

The sixth day we traveled about thirty miles, and had nothing to eat that day.

The seventh day we traveled about twenty-five miles; they killed a doe that day. She had two fawns in her, not yet haired. They stopped about four o'clock in the evening, and cooked the doe and her two fawns, and eat the whole up that night. They gave me part of a fawn to eat, but I could not eat it, it looked too tender. I eat part of the doe.

The eighth day we traveled about twenty-five miles, and had nothing to eat that day.

The ninth day we traveled about fifteen miles. We then arrived at an Indian hunting camp, where they made sugar that spring. About 11 o'clock in the forenoon, we had not yet anything to eat that day. The Indians that lived there had plenty of meat, hominy grease and sugar to eat. They gave us plenty of everything they had to eat. We were very hungry and ate like hungry dogs. When we were satisfied eating, the warriors went into a large cabin and I went with them, and immediately several of their friends came in to see them, both men and squaws, to hear the news. It is a custom with that nation for the squaws to demand presents of the warriors if they have been successful. After some little inquiry the squaws began to demand presents of the warriors; some would ask for a blanket, some for a shirt, some for a tomahawk; one squaw asked for a gun. The warriors never refused anything that was demanded. The manner in which they made their demand was, they would go up to an Indian and take hold of what they wanted. When the squaws were done with the warriors, there came a squaw and took hold of my blanket; I saw how the game was played, I just threw it off and gave it to her; then there came up a young squaw about eleven or twelve years old and took hold of my shirt, I did not want to let that go, as it was very cold day, and I let on I did not understand what she wanted. She appeared to be very much ashamed and went away. The older squaws encouraged and persuaded her to try it again; she came up the second time and took hold of my shirt again, I still pretended to be ignorant, but she held fast. I knew it would have to go. One of the warriors then stepped up and told me to let her have it. I then pulled it off and gave it to her. The old squaws laughed very much at the young squaw. I was then quite naked and it was a very cold day; I had nothing on me but moccasins, leggings and breachcloth. We remained there about 3 or 4 hours. The warriors then went out to the post to dance, they invited me to go with them to dance. I did so, they sung and danced around the war-post for half an hour. The old Indians would sing and dance sometimes out of the ring and appeared very lively. The warriors then marched right off from their dance on their journey. We had not got more than about 50 or 60 yards when I looked back and saw a squaw running with a blanket; she threw it on my shoulders, it fell down. I turned round and picked it up, it was a very old, dirty, lousy blanket, though it was better than nothing, as the day was very cold. We travelled about five or six miles that evening, then encamped in the woods. I suffered very much that night from the cold.

The tenth day we traveled five or six miles in the morning. We got within a quarter of a mile of a new town, on the west bank of the Wabash river, where those warriors resided, about nine o'clock, and made a halt at a running branch of water, where the timber was very thick, so that they could conceal themselves from the view of the town. Then they washed themselves all over and dressed themselves with paint of different colors. They made me wash, then they painted me and said I was a Kickapoo. Then they cut a pole and pealed it, painted it different colors and stuck the big end in the ground, and cleared a ring around the pole for to dance in. The fifth night they cut a lock of hair out of the crown of my head about as thick as my finger, plaited it elegantly and put it in their conjuring bag, and hung that bag on the pole they contemplated dancing around, and said that was their prisoner, and I was a Kickapoo, and must dance with them. When they all got ready to dance, the captain gave three very loud halloes, then walked into the ring and the rest all followed him. They placed me the third next to the captain; they then began to sing and dance. When we had danced about half an hour, I saw several old men, boys and squaws come running to where we were dancing. When there were a considerable number of them collected, the captain stepped out of the ring and spoke to the squaws. He told them to carry his and the other warriors' budgets to the town; the captain then joined the other warriors and me in the dancing ring; he marched in the front and we danced and sung all the way from there into the town. Some of the old Indian warriors marched upon each side of us, and at times would sing and dance until we got into their town. We continued dancing until we got through the town to the war-post, which stood on the west bank of the Wabash river; danced round that about twenty minutes; they then marched into the town, took all the cords off me, and showed me a cabin, told me to go in there, they were good Indians, they would give me something to eat; I need not fear, as they would not hurt me. I accordingly went in, where I received a plenty to eat and was treated very kindly. The warriors went into other cabins and feasted very greedily. We had not eat anything that morning nor the night before. About one hour and a half before the sun set the same evening, the warriors went out to the war-post again to dance. They took me with them; several other Indians were present. They had danced about half an hour when I saw two Indian men and a squaw riding a horseback across the Wabash river, from the east side; they came to where we were dancing. One of the Indians had a hand-kerchief tied around his head and was carrying a gun; the other had a cocked hat on his head, and had a large sword. The warriors never let on that they saw them, but continued dancing about fifteen minutes. After the two Indians and squaw came up the warriors quit dancing, and went to them and shook hands; they appeared very glad to see each other. The captain of the

13

warriors then talked with them about half an hour, and appeared to be very serious in their conversation. The captain then told me I must go with them two Indians and squaw. The sun was just then setting; the two Indians looked very much pleased. I did not want to go with them, as I knew not where they were going, and would have rather remained with the warriors that took me, as I had got acquainted with them, but the captain told me I must go with the two Indians and squaw, and that they were very good Indians. The Indian that had the sword rode up to a stump and told me to get up behind him on his horse; I did so with great reluctance, as I knew not where they were going; they looked very much like warriors. However, they started off very lively, and the Indian that I was riding behind began to plague and joke the squaw about me; she was his sister-in-law. He was an Indian that was full of life and very funny. When I got acquainted with him I was well pleased with him. We traveled about ten miles that evening before we reached the place they resided. They were then living at a sugar camp, where they had made sugar that spring, on the west bank of the Wabash, about ten miles below the old Kickapoos' trading town, opposite to the Weawes town. We arrived at their sugar camp about two hours in the night. They then gave me to an old Kickapoo chief, who was the father of the Indian that carried the gun, and the squaw, and the father-in-law of the funny Indian. The old chief soon began to inquire of me where I lived, and where the Indians caught me. I told him. He then asked me if they did not kill an Indian when they took me prisoner. I told him no, there was no body with me but one man and he had no gun. He then asked me again, if the Indians did not kill one of their own men when they took me. I told him I did not know; the captain told me they did, but I did not see them kill him. The old chief then told me that it was true, they did kill him, and said he was a bad Indian, he wanted to kill me. By this time the young squaw, the daughter of the old chief, whom I traveled in company with that evening, had prepared a good supper for me; it was hominy beat in a mortar, as white and as handsome as I ever saw, and well cooked; she fried some dried meat, pounded very fine in a mortar, in oil, then sprinkled sugar very plentifully over it. I ate very hearty; indeed, it was all very good and well cooked. When I was done eating, the old chief told me to eat more. I told him I had eat enough. He said no, if I did not eat more I could not live. Then the young squaw handed me a tin-cupful of water, sweetened with sugar. It relished very well. Then the old chief began to make further inquiries. He asked me if I had a wife and family. I told him I had a wife and three children. The old chief then appeared to be very sorry for my misfortune, and told me that I was among good Indians, I need not fear, they would not hurt me, and after awhile I should go home to my family; that I should go down the Wabash to Opost, from there down to the Ohio, then down the Ohio, and then up the Mississippi to Kaskaskia. We sat up until almost midnight; the old chief appeared very friendly indeed. The young squaw had prepared a very good bed for me, with bearskins and blankets. I laid down and slept very comfortably that night. It appeared as though I had got into another world, after being confined and tied down with so many ropes and the loss of sleep nine nights. I remained in bed pretty late next morning. I felt quite easy in mind, but my wrists and legs pained me very much and felt very sore. The young squaw had her breakfast prepared and I eat very hearty. When breakfast was over this funny Indian came over and took me to his cabin, about forty yards from the old chief's. There were none living at that place then but the old chief, his wife and daughter. They lived by themselves in one cabin and the old chief's son and son-in-law and their wives in another cabin, and a widow squaw, the old chief's daughter, lived by herself in a cabin adjoining her brother and brother-in-law. None of them had any children but the old chief. A few minutes after I went into this funny Indian's cabin he asked me if I wanted to shave. I told him yes, my beard was very long. He then got a razor and gave it to me. It was a very good one. I told him it wanted strapping. He went and brought his shot-pouch strap. He held one end and I the other end. I gave the razor a few passes on the strap, and found the razor to be a very good one. By this time the old chief's young squaw had come over; she immediately prepared some hot water for me to shave, and brought it in a tincup and gave it to me, and a piece of very good shaving soap. By the time I was done shaving the young squaw had prepared some clean water in a pewter basin for me to wash, and a cloth to wipe my hands and face. She then told me to sit down on a bench; I did so. She got two very good combs, a coarse and a fine one. It was then the fashion to wear long hair; my hair was very long and very thick and very much matted and tangled; I traveled without my hat or anything else on my head; that was the tenth day it had not been combed. She combed out my hair very tenderly, and then took the fine one and combed and looked over my head nearly one hour. She then went to a trunk and got a ribbon and queued my hair very nicely. The old chief's son then gave me a very good regimental blue cloth coat, faced with yellow buff-colored cloth. The son-in-law gave me a very good beaver macaroni hat. These they had taken from some officers they had killed. Then the widow squaw took me into her cabin and gave me a new ruffled shirt and a very good blanket. They told me to put them on; I did so. When I had got my fine dress on, the funny Indian told me to walk across the floor. I knew they wanted to have a little fun. I put my arms akimbo with my hands on my hips, and walked with a very proud air three or four times backwards and forwards across the floor. The funny Indian said in Indian that I was a very handsome man and a big captain. I then sat down, and they viewed me very much, and said I had a very handsome leg and thigh, and began to tell how fast I ran when the Indians caught me, and showed how I ran—like a bird flying. They appeared to be very well pleased with me, and I felt as comfortable as the nature of the case would admit of.

The next morning after breakfast, they all left that camp; they put all their property into a large perouge and moved by water up the Wabash river to the old Kickapoo trading town, about ten miles from their sugar camp; they sent me by land and one Indian with me. When we had got about half way to the town, we met with a young Frenchman; his name was Ebart; I was very well acquainted with him in the Illinois country; he spoke tolerably good English. The Indian then left me, and I went on to the town with the young Frenchman; I got to the town before the Indians arrived with their perouge, and the young Frenchman showed me their cabin, and told me to stay there until they would come, that they would be there in a few minutes. I there met with an English trader, a very friendly man, whose name was John McCauslin; he was from the north of England; we made some little acquaintance. He was a Freemason and appeared very sorry for my misfortune and told me he would do everything in his power to befriend me and told me I was with good Indians, they would not hurt me. He inquired of me where I lived and asked if I had a family. He then told me of the circumstance of the Indians killing one of their own men that day they caught me. He said it was a fact, he was a bad Indian and would not obey the commands of his captain and that he was still determined to kill me. My Indian family soon arrived and cleared up their cabin and got their family ready. They were a smart, neat and cleanly family, kept their cabin very nice and clean, the same as white women, and cooked their victuals very nice. After dinner was over, there came four Indians in the old chief's cabin. Two of them were the old chief's brother's children. They appeared to be in a very fine humor. I did not know but that they belonged to the same family and town. They had not been there more than one hour, until the old chief and the four Indians sat down on the floor in the cabin and had a long discourse about an hour and a half. Then all got up. The old chief then told me I must go with those Indians. I told him I did not want to go. He then told me I must go; that they were his children and that they were very good Indians; they would not hurt me. Then the old chief gave me to the oldest brother, in place of his father who was killed about one year before by the white people; he was one of their chiefs. Then the four Indians started off and I with them; they went down to the lower end of the town and stopped at an Indian cabin and got some bread and meat to eat. They gave me some. I did not go into the Indian cabin. They had not been in the cabin more than ten or twelve minutes before the old chief's young squaw came up and stood at the door. She would not go in. I discovered the Indians laughing and plaguing her. She looked in a very ill humor; she did not want them to take me away. They immediately started from the cabin and took a tolerably large path that led into the woods in a pretty smart trot. The squaw started immediately after them. They would look back once in a while, and when they would see the squaw coming they would whoop, hollow and laugh. When they got out of sight of the squaw they stopped running and traveled in a moderate walk. When we got about three miles from the town, they stopped where a large tree had fallen by the side of the path and laid high off the ground. They got up high on the log and looked back to see if the squaw was coming. When the squaw came up she stopped and they began to plague her and laugh at her. They spoke in English. They talked very vulgar to the squaw. She soon began to cry. When they got tired plaguing her, they jumped off the log and started on their road in a trot, and I ran with them. The squaw stood still till we got most out of sight. They would look back and laugh and some-times hollow and whoop, and appeared to be very much diverted. They did not run very far before they slackened in their runnings. They then walked moderately until they got to their town, which was three miles further from the tree they stopped at. We got into their town about one hour and a half before the sun set. That same evening the squaw came in about half an hour after we arrived. I met with a young man that evening who had been taken prisoner about eighteen months before I was taken. His name was Nicholas Coonse (a Dutchman), then about 19 years of age. He heard I was coming, and he came to meet me a little way out of town. He was very glad to see me and I to see him, and we soon made up acquaintance. Coonse and myself were to live in one cabin together. The two brothers that I was given up to, one of them claimed Coonse and the other claimed me. They both lived in the same cabin. When the squaw arrived, she came immediately to our cabin and stood outside at the door; she would not come in. I noticed the Indians plaguing and laughing at her; she looked very serious. About sunset, Coonse asked me if I wanted a wife. (He could not speak very good English, but he could speak pretty good Indian.) I told him no. He then told me if I wanted one I could have one. I asked him how he knew that. He said, "There is a squaw that wants to marry you," pointing at her. I told him I reckoned not. He says, "Yes. Indeed, she tus; she came after you a purpose to marry you."

18

I told Coonse I had a wife, and I did not want another one. He says, "O, well, if you want her you can haf her." She stood by the door for some time after dark. I did not know when she went away; she said two days and three nights before she returned home. I never spoke a word to her while she was there. She was a very handsome girl, about 18 years of age, a beautiful, full figure and handsomely featured, and very white for a squaw. She was almost as white as dark complexioned white women generally are. Her father and mother were very white skinned Indians.

The next day was the 9th day of April, and thirteenth day that I had been their prisoner. The chief Indians and warriors that day held a general council, to know in what manner and way to dispose of me. They collected in the cabin where I lived. While they were in council their dinner was cooking. There were about ten in number, and they all sat down on the floor in a circle, and then commenced by their interpreter, Nicholas Coonse.

The first question they asked me was, "Would I have my hair cut off like they cut theirs?" I answered "No." The second question they asked me was, "If I would have holes bored in my ears and nose and have rings and lead hung in them like they had?" I answered "No." The third question they asked me was, "If I could make hats?" (I had a large bag of beaver fur with me when they took me prisoner; from that circumstance I suppose they thought I was a hatter.) I answered "No." The fourth question they asked me was, "If I was a carpenter?" and said they wanted a door made for their cabin. I answered "No." The fifth question they asked me was, "If I was a blacksmith; could I mend their guns and makes axes and hoes for them?" I answered "No." The sixth question they asked me was, "If I could hoe corn?" I answered "No". The seventh question they asked me was, "If I could hunt?" I answered. "No. I could shoot at a mark very well, but I never hunted any." Then they told Coonse to ask me how I got my living; if I could do no work. I thought I had out-generalled them, but that question stumped me a little. The first thought that struck my mind, I thought I would tell them I was a weaver by trade, but a second thought occurred to my

19

mind, I told Coonse to tell them I made my living by writing. The Indians answered and said it was very well. The eighth question they asked me was, "If I had a family?" I answered "Yes, I had a wife and three children." The ninth question they asked me was, "If I wanted to go home to see my wife and children?" I answered "Yes," They said, "Very well, you shall go home by and by." The tenth question they asked was, "If I wanted a wife then?" I answered "No," and told them it was not the fashion for the white people to have two wives at the same time. They said, very well, I could get one if I wanted one, and they said if I staid with them until their corn got in roasting ears, then I must take a wife. I answered them yes, if I staid that long with them. They then told me that I might go anywhere about in the town, but not go out of sight of the town, for if I did, there were bad Indians round about the town and they would catch me and kill me, and they said they could run like horses; and another thing they said, don't you recollect the Indians that took you prisoner and cut a lock of hair out of the crown of your head. I told them yes. Then they told me in consequence of that, if you attempted to run away, you could not live eight days. If you will stay with us and not run away, you shall not even bring water to drink. I told them I wanted to go home to my family, but I would not go without letting them know before I went. They said, very well. They appeared well pleased with me and told me again I might go anywhere about in the town, but not go out of sight of the town. I was sitting on a bench, when the old chief got up and put both his hands on my head and said something, I did not know what. Then he gave me a name and called me "Mohcossea," after the old chief that was killed, who was the father of the Indian that I was given up to. Then I was considered one of that family, a Kickapoo in place of their father, the old chief. Then the principal chief took the peace pipe and smoked two or three draws. It had a long stem about three feet in length. He then passed it round to the other Indians before they raised from their council. He held the pipe by the end and each of them took two or three draws. Then he handed it to me and I smoked. The chief then said I was a Kickapoo and that they were good Indians and that I need not be afraid; they would not hurt me, but I must not run away.

By this time their dinner was prepared and they were ready to eat. They all sat down and told me to sit by. I did, and we all eat a hearty dinner and they all appeared to be well pleased with their new adopted Kickapoo brother.

These Indians lived about six miles west of the old Kickapoo trading town, on the west side of the Wabash river. They had no traders in their town. After dinner was over, they told the interpreter Coons that I must write to their trading town for some bread. I told Coons to tell them I had nothing to write with—no paper, nor pen and ink. They said I must write. I told Coons to tell them again I had no paper nor nothing to write with. Coons told them. Then the Indian that claimed me went to his trunk and brought me a letter that had one-half sheet of it clean paper. I told Coons to tell them I wanted a pen. The same Indian went and pulled a quill out of a turkey wing and gave it to me. I told Coons I wanted a knife to make the pen. The same Indian got his scalping knife; he gave it two or three little whets and gave it to me. I then told Coons I wanted some ink. Coons says, "Ink—ink; what is tat? I ton't know what ink is." He had no name for ink in Indian or English. I told him to tell the Indian to get me some gunpowder and water and a spoon and I would make the ink myself. The Indian did so. I knew very well what their drift was; they wanted a proof to know whether I told them any lies when they examined me in their council. When I had made the ink and was ready to write I asked Coons how many loaves of bread I should write for. He says, "Ho! a couple of lofes; tay only want to know if you can write or if you told them any lies or not." I wrote to the English trader, that I mentioned before that I had made some acquaintance with the day I passed the old trading town, for to get me two loaves of bread. He very well knew my situation and circumstances. There was a Frenchman, a baker, that lived in the trading town.

When I had finished writing, the Indian took it up and looked at it and said, "Depaway, vely good." Coons' master, a brother to the one that claimed me, told Coons to go catch his horse and take the letter for the bread, not stay, but return as soon as possible. Coons hurried off immediately and soon returned. As soon as he came back he brought the two loaves of bread and gave them to me. I then asked Coons what I should do with this bread, as he was somewhat better acquainted with the ways of the Indians than I was. He says, "Kife one loaf to tay old squaw and her two little chiltren, and tofide the otter loaf petween you and your master, put keep a pigest half." I did so. This old squaw was the mother of the two Indians that claimed Coons and myself. The old squaw and her two children soon eat their loaf. I then divided my half between the two little children again. That pleased the old squaw very much; she tried to make me sensible of her thanks for my kindness to her two little children.

While Coons was gone for the bread, the Indian that claimed me asked me to write his name. I asked him to speak his name distinctly. He did. I had heard it spoken several times before. His name was "Mahtomack." When I was done writing he took it up and looked at it and said it was "Depaway." He then went to his trunk and brought his powder horn, which had his name wrote on it by an officer at Post Vincennes in large print letters, and compared them together. They both were the same kind of letters and his name spelt exactly the same. He seemed mightily pleased and said it was "bon vely good." It was a big captain he said wrote his name on the powder-horn at Opost. The wife of the Indian that claimed me, next morning combed and queued my hair and gave me a very large ostrich feather and tied it to my hat. The Sunday following after I was taken to that town, there was a number of Indians went from that town to the old Kickapoo trading town. They took me with them to dance what is called the "Beggar's Dance." It is a practice for the Indians every spring, when they come in from their hunting ground, to go to the trading towns and dance for presents; they will go through the streets and dance before all the traders' doors. The traders then will give them presents, such as tobacco, bread, knives, spirits, blankets, tomahawks, &c.

While we were in town that day I talked with my friend McCauslin to speak to the Indians and try to get them to sell me, but they would not agree to sell me then. They said they would come down the Sunday following and bring me with them, perhaps they would then agree to sell me. They complied with their promise and brought me down with them. My friend McCauslin then inquired of them if they had agreed to sell me; they told him they would. McCauslin then sent for the interpreter, and the Indians asked one hundred buckskins for me in merchandize. The interpreter asked me if I would give it? I told him I would. The Indians then went to the traders' houses to receive their pay. They took but seventy bucks' worth of merchandize at that time. One of the articles they took was bread, three loaves, one for the Indian that claimed me, one for his wife, the other one for me. I saw directly they wanted me to go back home with them. After a little while they started and motioned and told me I must go with them. I refused to go. The Indian fellow took hold of my arm and tried to pull me forward. I still refused going with them. He still continued pulling and his wife pushing me at the back. We went scuffling along a few yards till we got before my friend McCauslin's cabin door. He discovered the bustle and asked me what the Indians wanted. I told him they wanted me to go home with them. He asked me if I wanted to go. I told him no. He then told me to walk into his cabin and sit down and he would go and bring the interpreter. I went in and the two Indians followed me into the cabin and sat down. The interpreter came in immediately and asked the Indians what they wanted. They told him they wanted me to go home with them. The interpreter then asked if I wanted to go with them. I told him no. He then told the Indians they had sold me and that they had nothing more to do with me, that I was a freeman, that I might stay where I pleased. They then said they had not received all their pay. The interpreter then asked them why they did not take it all? They said they expected I would go home with them and remain with them until I got an opportunity to go home. The interpreter then told them they could get the balance of their pay. They said if I did not go home with them they must have thirty bucks more. The interpreter asked me if I was willing to give it. I told him yes. I did not want to go back again. The Indians then went and took their thirty dollars of balance and thirty more and went off home. I then owed the traders that advanced the goods for me one hundred and thirty buckskins for my ransom, which they considered equal to $260 in silver. There were five traders that were concerned in the payment of the goods to the Indians. One of them was a Mr. Bazedone a Spaniard, who sometimes traded in the Illinois country, with whom I had some acquaintance. I told him if he would satisfy the other four traders, I would give him my note, payable in the Illinois country. He did so, and I gave him my note for the $260, to be paid twelve months after date in the Illinois country, and $37 more for my boarding and necessaries I could not do without, such as a bear skin and blanket to sleep on, a shirt, hat, tobacco and handkerchief.

My friend McCauslin took me to a Frenchman's house—he was a baker by trade, the only baker in town—to board with him until I got an opportunity to go home. Two days after I went to stay at the baker's, the Indian that claimed me, his squaw and the young squaw that followed us to the new town, came to see me and stayed three or four hours with me. He asked me to give him some tobacco. I told him I had no money. He thought I could get anything I wanted. I bought him a carrot of tobacco; it weighed about three pounds; he seemed very well pleased. He and his wife wanted me very much to go back home with them again. I told them I could not, that I was very anxious to go home to my wife and family. Three or four days after that they revisited me, and still insisted on me to go home with them. I told them that I expected every day to get an opportunity to go home. I had some doubts about going back with them; I thought perhaps they might play some trick on me, and take me to some other town; and their water was so bad I could not drink it—nothing but a small pond to make use of for their drinking and cooking, about forty or fifty yards long and about thirty yards wide. Their horses would not only drink from, but wallow in it; the little Indian boys every day would swim in it, and the Indians soak their deerskins in it. I could not bear to drink it. When they would bring in a kettle of water to drink, they would set it down on the floor. The dogs would generally took the first drink out of the kettle. I have often seen when the dogs would be drinking out of a kettle, an Indian would go up and kick him off, and take up the kettle and drink after the dog. They had nothing to eat the last week I was with them but Indian potatoes—some people call them hoppines—that grew in the woods, and they were very scarce. Sometimes the Indian boys would catch land terrapins. They would draw their heads out and tie a string around their neck and hang them up a few minutes, and then put them in a kettle of water with some corn—when they had it—without taking the entrails out or shell off the terrapin, and eat the soup as well as the meat. We had all liked to have starved that week; we had no meat; I was glad to get away.

I staid three weeks with the French baker before I got an opportunity to start home. I had a plenty to eat while I remained with the baker—good light bread, bacon and sandy hill cranes, boiled in leyed corn, which made a very good soup. I paid him three dollars per week for my board.

There was a Mr. Pyatt a Frenchman, and his wife, whose residence was at St. Vincennes, with whom I had some acquaintance. They had moved up to that Kickapoo town in the fall of the year in order to trade with the Indians that winter. They were then ready to return home to Vincennes. Mr. Pyatt had purchased a drove of horses from the Indians. He had to go by land with his horses. Mrs. Pyatt hired a large perogue and four Frenchmen to take her property home to Vincennes. I got a passage in her perogue. She was very friendly to me; she did not charge me anything for my passage.

We arrived in Vincennes in forty-eight hours after we left the Kickapoo trading town, which is said to be two hundred and ten miles. The river was very high, and the four hands rowed day and night. We never put to land but twice to get a little wood to cook something to eat.

I staid five days at Vincennes before I got an opportunity of company to go on my way home. It was too dangerous for one man to travel alone by land without a gun. There was a Mr. Duff, who lived in the Illinois country, came to Vincennes to move a

Mrs. Moredock and family to the Illinois. I got a passage with him by water. The morning I started from Vincennes he was just ready to start before I knew I could get a passage with him, and I had not time to write. I got a Mr. John Rice Jones, a friend of mine, to write to Col. Edgar, living in Kaskaskia, in the Illinois, who was a particular friend of mine, and sent it by the express, a Frenchman, that was going to start that day from Vincennes to Kaskaskia, which he could ride in four days, and request Col. Edgar to write to my wife, who lived at Bellfontain, about forty miles from Kaskaskia, and inform her that I was at Post Vin-cennes, on my return home with a Mr. Duff by water, and inform her that I would be at Kaskaskia on a certain day; I think it was two weeks from the time I left Vincennes, and for her to send me a horse on that day to Kaskaskia. Col. Edgar wrote to her imme-diately, as soon as he received Mr. Jones' letter. That was the first time she heard from me after I was taken prisoner. I had written to her while I was at the Kickapoo town. That letter never reached her. I had two brothers living at the Bellfontain; they met me on the day I proposed being at Kaskaskia and brought me a horse. The next day I got home to the Bellfontain.

Narrative
of the Captivity
and Restoration of
Mrs. Mary Rowlandson

Narrative of
Mrs. Mary Rowlandson

The sovereignty and goodness of GOD, together with the faithfulness of his promises displayed, being a narrative of the captivity and restoration of Mrs. Mary Rowlandson, commended by her, to all that desires to know the Lord's doings to, and dealings with her. Especially to her dear children and relations. The second Addition [sic] Corrected and amended. Written by her own hand for her private use, and now made public at the earnest desire of some friends, and for the benefit of the afflicted. Deut. 32.39. See now that I, even I am he, and there is no god with me, I kill and I make alive, I wound and I heal, neither is there any can deliver out of my hand.

On the tenth of February 1675, came the Indians with great numbers upon Lancaster: their first coming was about sunrising; hearing the noise of some guns, we looked out; several houses were burning, and the smoke ascending to heaven. There were five persons taken in one house; the father, and the mother and a sucking child, they knocked on the head; the other two they took and carried away alive. There were two others, who being out of their garrison upon some occasion were set upon; one was knocked on the head, the other escaped; another there was who running along was shot and wounded, and fell down; he begged of them his life, promising them money (as they told me) but they would not hearken to him but knocked him in head, and stripped him naked, and split open his bowels. Another, seeing many of the Indians about his barn, ventured and went out, but was quickly shot down. There were three others belonging to the same garrison who were killed; the Indians getting up upon the roof of the barn, had advantage to shoot down upon them over their fortification. Thus these murderous wretches went on, burning, and destroying before them.

At length they came and beset our own house, and quickly it was the dolefulest day that ever mine eyes saw. The house stood upon the edge of a hill; some of the Indians got behind the hill, others into the barn, and others behind anything that could shelter them; from all which places they shot against the house, so that the bullets seemed to fly like hail; and quickly they wounded one man among us, then another, and then a third. About two hours (according to my observation, in that amazing time) they had been about the house before they prevailed to fire it (which they did with flax and hemp, which they brought out of the barn, and there being no defense about the house, only two flankers at two opposite corners and one of them not finished); they fired it once and one ventured out and quenched it, but they quickly fired it again, and that took. Now is the dreadful hour come, that I have often heard of (in time of war, as it was the case of others), but now mine eyes see it. Some in our house were fighting for their lives, others wallowing in their blood, the house on fire over our heads, and the bloody heathen ready to knock us on the head, if we stirred out. Now might we hear mothers and children crying out for themselves, and one another, "Lord, what shall we do?" Then I took my children (and one of my sisters', hers) to go forth and leave the house: but as soon as we came to the door and appeared, the Indians shot so thick that the bullets rattled against the house, as if one had taken an handful of stones and threw them, so that we were fain to give back. We had six stout dogs belonging to our garrison, but none of them would stir, though another time, if any Indian had come to the door, they were ready to fly upon him and tear him down. The Lord hereby would make us the more acknowledge His hand, and to see that our help is always in Him. But out we must go, the fire increasing, and coming along behind us, roaring, and the Indians gaping before us with their guns, spears, and hatchets to devour us. No sooner were we out of the house, but my brother-in-law (being before wounded, in defending the house, in or near the throat) fell down dead, whereat the Indians scornfully shouted, and hallowed, and were presently upon him, stripping off his clothes, the bullets flying thick, one went through my side, and the same (as would seem) through the bowels and hand of my dear child in my arms. One of my elder sisters' children, named William, had then his leg broken, which the Indians perceiving, they knocked him on [his] head. Thus were we butchered by those merciless heathen, standing amazed, with the blood running down to our heels. My eldest sister being yet in the house, and seeing those woeful sights, the infidels hauling mothers one way, and children another, and some wallowing in their blood: and her elder son telling her that her son William was dead, and myself was wounded, she said, "And Lord, let me die with them," which was no sooner said, but she was struck with a bullet, and fell down dead over the threshold. I hope she is reaping the fruit of her good labors, being faithful to the service of God in her place. In her younger years she lay under much trouble upon spiritual accounts, till it pleased God to make that precious scripture take hold of her heart, "And he said unto me, my Grace is sufficient for thee" (2 Corinthians 12.9). More than twenty years after, I have heard her tell how sweet and comfortable that place was to her. But to return: the Indians laid hold of us, pulling me one way, and the children another, and said, "Come go along with us"; I told them they would kill me: they answered, if I were willing to go along with them, they would not hurt me.

Oh the doleful sight that now was to behold at this house! "Come, behold the works of the Lord, what desolations he has made in the earth." Of thirty-seven persons who were in this one house, none escaped either present death, or a bitter captivity, save only one, who might say as he, "And I only am escaped alone to tell the News" (Job 1.15). There were twelve killed, some shot, some stabbed with their spears, some knocked down with their hatchets. When we are in prosperity, Oh the little that we think of such dreadful sights, and to see our dear friends, and relations lie bleeding out their heart-blood upon the ground. There was one who was chopped into the head with a hatchet, and stripped naked, and yet was crawling up and down. It is a solemn sight to see so many Christians lying in their blood, some here, and some there, like a company of sheep torn by wolves, all of them stripped naked by a company of hell-hounds, roaring, singing, ranting, and insulting, as if they would have torn our very hearts out; yet the Lord by His almighty power preserved a number of us from death, for there were twenty-four of us taken alive and carried captive.

I had often before this said that if the Indians should come, I should choose rather to be killed by them than taken alive, but when it came to the trial my mind changed; their glittering weapons so daunted my spirit, that I chose rather to go along with those (as I may say) ravenous beasts, than that moment to end my days; and that I may the better declare what happened to me during that grievous captivity, I shall particularly speak of the several removes we had up and down the wilderness.

THE FIRST REMOVE

Now away we must go with those barbarous creatures, with our bodies wounded and bleeding, and our hearts no less than our bodies. About a mile we went that night, up upon a hill within sight of the town, where they intended to lodge. There was hard by a vacant house (deserted by the English before, for fear of the Indians). I asked them whether I might not lodge in the house that night, to which they answered, "What, will you love English men still?" This was the dolefulest night that ever my eyes saw. Oh the roaring, and singing and dancing, and yelling of those black creatures in the night, which made the place a lively resemblance of hell. And as miserable was the waste that was there made of horses, cattle, sheep, swine, calves, lambs, roasting pigs, and fowl (which they had plundered in the town), some roasting, some lying and burning, and some boiling to feed our merciless enemies; who were joyful enough, though we were disconsolate. To add to the dolefulness of the former day, and the dismalness of the present night, my thoughts ran upon my losses and sad bereaved condition. All was gone, my husband gone (at least separated from me, he being in the Bay; and to add to my grief, the Indians told me they would kill him as he came homeward), my children gone, my relations and friends gone, our house and home and all our comforts—within door and without—all was gone (except my life), and I knew not but the next moment that might go too. There remained nothing to me but one poor wounded babe, and it seemed at present worse than death that it was in such a pitiful condition, bespeaking compassion, and I had no refreshing for it, nor suitable things to revive it. Little do many think what is the savageness and brut-ishness of this barbarous enemy, Ay, even those that seem to profess more than others among them, when the English have fallen into their hands.

Those seven that were killed at Lancaster the summer be-fore upon a Sabbath day, and the one that was afterward killed upon a weekday, were slain and mangled in a barbarous manner, by one-eyed John, and Marlborough's Praying Indians, which Capt. Mosely brought to Boston, as the Indians told me.

THE SECOND REMOVE

But now, the next morning, I must turn my back upon the town, and travel with them into the vast and desolate wilder-ness, I knew not whither. It is not my tongue, or pen, can express the sorrows of my heart, and bitterness of my spirit that I had at this departure: but God was with me in a wonderful manner, carrying me along, and bearing up my spirit, that it did not quite fail. One of the Indians carried my poor wounded babe upon a horse; it went moaning all along, "I shall die, I shall die." I went on foot after it, with sorrow that cannot be expressed. At length I took it off the horse, and carried it in my arms till my strength failed, and I fell down with it. Then they set me upon a horse with my wounded child in my lap, and there being no furniture upon the horse's back, as we were going down a steep hill we both fell over the horse's head, at which they, like inhumane creatures, laughed, and rejoiced to see it, though I thought we should there have ended our days, as overcome with so many difficulties. But the Lord renewed my strength still, and carried me along, that I might see more of His power; yea, so much that I could never have thought of, had I not experienced it.

After this it quickly began to snow, and when night came on, they stopped, and now down I must sit in the snow, by a little fire, and a few boughs behind me, with my sick child in my lap; and calling much for water, being now (through the wound) fallen into a violent fever. My own wound also growing so stiff that I could scarce sit down or rise up; yet so it must be, that I must sit all this cold winter night upon the cold snowy ground, with my sick child in my arms, looking that every hour would be the last of its life; and having no Christian friend near me, either to comfort or help me. Oh, I may see the wonderful power of God, that my Spirit did not utterly sink under my affliction: still the Lord upheld me with His gracious and merciful spirit, and we were both alive to see the light of the next morning.

THE THIRD REMOVE

The morning being come, they prepared to go on their way. One of the Indians got up upon a horse, and they set me up behind him, with my poor sick babe in my lap. A very wearisome and tedious day I had of it; what with my own wound, and my child's being so exceeding sick, and in a lamentable condition with her wound. It may be easily judged what a poor feeble condition we were in, there being not the least crumb of refreshing that came within either of our mouths from Wednesday night to Saturday night, except only a little cold water. This day in the afternoon, about an hour by sun, we came to the place where they intended, viz. an Indian town, called Wenimesset, northward of Quabaug. When we were come, Oh the number of pagans (now merciless enemies) that there came about me, that I may say as David, "I had fainted, unless I had believed, etc" (Psalm 27.13). The next day was the Sabbath. I then remembered how careless I had been of God's holy time; how many Sabbaths I had lost and misspent, and how evilly I had walked in God's sight; which lay so close unto my spirit, that it was easy for me to see how righteous it was with God to cut off the thread of my life and cast me out of His presence forever. Yet the Lord still showed mercy to me, and upheld me; and as He wounded me with one hand, so he healed me with the other. This day there came to me one Robert Pepper (a man belonging to Roxbury) who was taken in Captain Beers's fight, and had been now a considerable time with the Indians; and up with them almost as far as Albany, to see King Philip, as he told me, and was now very lately come into these parts. Hearing, I say, that I was in this Indian town, he obtained leave to come and see me. He told me he himself was wounded in the leg at Captain Beer's fight; and was not able some time to go, but as they carried him, and as he took oaken leaves and laid to his wound, and through the blessing of God he was able to travel again. Then I took oaken leaves and laid to my side, and with the blessing of God it cured me also; yet before the cure was wrought, I may say, as it is in Psalm 38.5-6 "My wounds stink and are corrupt, I am troubled, I am bowed down greatly, I go mourning all the day long." I sat much alone with a poor wounded child in my lap, which moaned night and day, having nothing to revive the body, or cheer the spirits of her, but instead of that, sometimes one Indian would come and tell me one hour that "your master will knock your child in the head," and then a second, and then a third, "your master will quickly knock your child in the head."

This was the comfort I had from them, miserable comforters are ye all, as he said. Thus nine days I sat upon my knees, with my babe in my lap, till my flesh was raw again; my child being even ready to depart this sorrowful world, they bade me carry it out to another wigwam (I suppose because they would not be troubled with such spectacles) whither I went with a very heavy heart, and down I sat with the picture of death in my lap. About two hours in the night, my sweet babe like a lamb departed this life on Feb. 18, 1675. It being about six years, and five months old. It was nine days from the first wounding, in this miserable condition, without any refreshing of one nature or other, except a little cold water. I cannot but take notice how at another time I could not bear to be in the room where any dead person was, but now the case is changed; I must and could lie down by my dead babe, side by side all the night after. I have thought since of the wonderful goodness of God to me in preserving me in the use of my reason and senses in that distressed time, that I did not use wicked and violent means to end my own miserable life. In the morning, when they understood that my child was dead they sent for me home to my master's wigwam (by my master in this writing, must be understood Quinnapin, who was a Saga-more, and married King Philip's wife's sister; not that he first took me, but I was sold to him by another Narragansett Indian, who took me when first I came out of the garrison). I went to take up my dead child in my arms to carry it with me, but they bid me let it alone; there was no resisting, but go I must and leave it. When I had been at my master's wigwam, I took the first opportunity I could get to go look after my dead child. When I came I asked them what they had done with it; then they told me it was upon the hill. Then they went and showed me where it was, where I saw the ground was newly digged, and there they told me they had buried it. There I left that child in the wilderness, and must commit it, and myself also in this wil-derness condition, to Him who is above all. God having taken away this dear child, I went to see my daughter Mary, who was at this same Indian town, at a wigwam not very far off, though we had little liberty or opportunity to see one another. She was about ten years old, and taken from the door at first by a Praying Ind. and afterward sold for a gun. When I came in sight, she would fall aweeping; at which they were provoked, and would not let me come near her, but bade me be gone; which was a heart-cutting word to me. I had one child dead, another in the wilderness, I knew not where, the third they would not let me come near to: "Me (as he said) have ye bereaved of my Children, Joseph is not, and Simeon is not, and ye will take Benjamin also, all these things are against me." I could not sit still in this condition, but kept walking from one place to another. And as I was going along, my heart was even overwhelmed with the thoughts of my condition, and that I should have children, and a nation which I knew not, ruled over them. Whereupon I earnestly entreated the Lord, that He would consider my low estate, and show me a token for good, and if it were His blessed will, some sign and hope of some relief. And indeed quickly the Lord answered, in some measure, my poor prayers; for as I was going up and down mourning and lamenting my condition, my son came to me, and asked me how I did. I had not seen him before, since the destruction of the town, and I knew not where he was, till I was informed by himself, that he was amongst a smaller parcel of Indians, whose place was about six miles off. With tears in his eyes, he asked me whether his sister Sarah was dead; and told me he had seen his sister Mary; and prayed me, that I would not be troubled in reference to himself. The occasion of his coming to see me at this time, was this: there was, as I said, about six miles from us, a small plantation of Indians, where it seems he had been during his captivity; and at this time, there were some forces of the Ind. gathered out of our company, and some also from them (among whom was my son's master) to go to assault and burn Medfield. In this time of the absence of his master, his dame brought him to see me. I took this to be some gracious answer to my earnest and unfeigned desire. The next day, viz. to this, the Indians returned from Medfield, all the company, for those that belonged to the other small company, came through the town that now we were at. But before they came to us, Oh! the outrageous roaring and hooping that there was. They began their din about a mile before they came to us. By their noise and hooping they signified how many they had destroyed (which was at that time twenty-three). Those that were with us at home were gathered together as soon as they heard the hooping, and every time that the other went over their number, these at home gave a shout, that the very earth rung again. And thus they continued till those that had been upon the expedition were come up to the Sagamore's wigwam; and then, Oh, the hideous insulting and triumphing that there was over some English-men's scalps that they had taken (as their manner is) and brought with them. I cannot but take notice of the wonderful mercy of God to me in those afflictions, in sending me a Bible. One of the Indians that came from Medfield fight, had brought some plunder, came to me, and asked me, if I would have a Bible, he had got one in his basket. I was glad of it, and asked him, whether he thought the Indians would let me read? He an- swered, yes. So I took the Bible, and in that melancholy time, it came into my mind to read first the 28th chapter of Deuteron- omy, which I did, and when I had read it, my dark heart wrought on this manner: that there was no mercy for me, that the blessings were gone, and the curses come in their room, and that I had lost my opportunity. But the Lord helped me still to go on reading till I came to Chap. 30, the seven first verses, where I found, there was mercy promised again, if we would re- turn to Him by repentance; and though we were scattered from one end of the earth to the other, yet the Lord would gather us together, and turn all those curses upon our enemies. I do not desire to live to forget this Scripture, and what comfort it was to me.

Now the Ind. began to talk of removing from this place, some one way, and some another. There were now besides my- self nine English captives in this place (all of them children, except one woman). I got an opportunity to go and take my leave of them. They being to go one way, and I another, I asked them whether they were earnest with God for deliverance. They told me they did as they were able, and it was some comfort to me, that the Lord stirred up children to look to Him. The woman, viz. goodwife Joslin, told me she should never see me again, and that she could find in her heart to run away. I wished her not to run away by any means, for we were near thirty miles from any English town, and she very big with child, and had but one week to reckon, and another child in her arms, two years old, and bad rivers there were to go over, and we were feeble, with our poor and coarse entertainment. I had my Bible with me, I pulled it out, and asked her whether she would read. We opened the Bible and lighted on Psalm 27, in which Psalm we especially took notice of that, ver. ult., "Wait on the Lord, Be of good courage, and he shall strengthen thine Heart, wait I say on the Lord."

THE FOURTH REMOVE

And now I must part with that little company I had. Here I parted from my daughter Mary (whom I never saw again till I saw her in Dorchester, returned from captivity), and from four little cousins and neighbors, some of which I never saw afterward: the Lord only knows the end of them. Amongst them also was that poor woman before mentioned, who came to a sad end, as some of the company told me in my travel: she having much grief upon her spirit about her miserable condition, being so near her time, she would be often asking the Indians to let her go home; they not being willing to that, and yet vexed with her importunity, gathered a great company together about her and stripped her naked, and set her in the midst of them, and when they had sung and danced about her (in their hellish manner) as long as they pleased they knocked her on head, and the child in her arms with her. When they had done that they made a fire and put them both into it, and told the other children that were with them that if they attempted to go home, they would serve them in like manner. The children said she did not shed one tear, but prayed all the while. But to return to my own journey, we traveled about half a day or little more, and came to a desolate place in the wilderness, where there were no wigwams or in-habitants before; we came about the middle of the afternoon to this place, cold and wet, and snowy, and hungry, and weary, and no refreshing for man but the cold ground to sit on, and our poor Indian cheer.

Heart-aching thoughts here I had about my poor children, who were scattered up and down among the wild beasts of the forest. My head was light and dizzy (either through hunger or hard lodging, or trouble or all together), my knees feeble, my body raw by sitting double night and day, that I cannot express to man the affliction that lay upon my spirit, but the Lord helped me at that time to express it to Himself. I opened my Bible to read, and the Lord brought that precious Scripture to me. "Thus saith the Lord, refrain thy voice from weeping, and thine eyes from tears, for thy work shall be rewarded, and they shall come again from the land of the enemy" (Jeremiah 31.16). This was a sweet cordial to me when I was ready to faint; many and many a time have I sat down and wept sweetly over this Scripture. At this place we continued about four days.

THE FIFTH REMOVE

The occasion (as I thought) of their moving at this time was the English army, it being near and following them. For they went as if they had gone for their lives, for some considerable way, and then they made a stop, and chose some of their stoutest men, and sent them back to hold the English army in play whilst the rest escaped. And then, like Jehu, they marched on furiously, with their old and with their young: some carried their old decrepit mothers, some carried one, and some another. Four of them carried a great Indian upon a bier; but going through a thick wood with him, they were hindered, and could make no haste, whereupon they took him upon their backs, and carried him, one at a time, till they came to Banquaug river. Upon a Friday, a little after noon, we came to this river. When all the company was come up, and were gathered together, I thought to count the number of them, but they were so many, and being somewhat in motion, it was beyond my skill. In this travel, because of my wound, I was somewhat favored in my load; I carried only my knitting work and two quarts of parched meal. Being very faint I asked my mistress to give me one spoonful of the meal, but she would not give me a taste. They quickly fell to cutting dry trees, to make rafts to carry them over the river: and soon my turn came to go over. By the advantage of some brush which they had laid upon the raft to sit upon, I did not wet my foot (which many of themselves at the other end were mid-leg deep) which cannot but be acknowledged as a favor of God to my weakened body, it being a very cold time. I was not before acquainted with such kind of doings or dangers. "When thou passeth through the waters I will be with thee, and through the rivers they shall not overflow thee" (Isaiah 43.2). A certain number of us got over the river that night, but it was the night after the Sabbath before all the company was got over. On the Saturday they boiled an old horse's leg which they had got, and so we drank of the broth, as soon as they thought it was ready, and when it was almost all gone, they filled it up again.

The first week of my being among them I hardly ate any thing; the second week I found my stomach grow very faint for want of something; and yet it was very hard to get down their filthy trash; but the third week, though I could think how formerly my stomach would turn against this or that, and I could starve and die before I could eat such things, yet they were sweet and savory to my taste. I was at this time knitting a pair of white cotton stockings for my mistress; and had not yet wrought upon a Sabbath day. When the Sabbath came they bade me go to work. I told them it was the Sabbath day, and desired them to let me rest, and told them I would do as much more tomorrow; to which they answered me they would break my face. And here I cannot but take notice of the strange providence of God in preserving the heathen. They were many hundreds, old and young, some sick, and some lame; many had papooses at their backs. The greatest number at this time with us were squaws, and they traveled with all they had, bag and baggage, and yet they got over this river aforesaid; and on Monday they set their wigwams on fire, and away they went. On that very day came the English army after them to this river, and saw the smoke of their wigwams, and yet this river put a stop to them. God did not give them courage or activity to go over after us. We were not ready for so great a mercy as victory and deliverance. If we had been God would have found out a way for the English to have passed this river, as well as for the Indians with their squaws and children, and all their luggage. "Oh that my people had hearkened to me, and Israel had walked in my ways, I should soon have subdued their enemies, and turned my hand against their adversaries" (Psalm 81.13-14).

THE SIXTH REMOVE

On Monday (as I said) they set their wigwams on fire and went away. It was a cold morning, and before us there was a great brook with ice on it; some waded through it, up to the knees and higher, but others went till they came to a beaver dam, and I amongst them, where through the good providence of God, I did not wet my foot. I went along that day mourning and lamenting, leaving farther my own country, and traveling into a vast and howling wilderness, and I understood something of Lot's wife's temptation, when she looked back. We came that day to a great swamp, by the side of which we took up our lodging that night. When I came to the brow of the hill, that looked toward the swamp, I thought we had been come to a great Indian town (though there were none but our own company). The Indians were as thick as the trees: it seemed as if there had been a thousand hatchets going at once. If one looked before one there was nothing but Indians, and behind one, nothing but Indians, and so on either hand, I myself in the midst, and no Christian soul near me, and yet how hath the Lord preserved me in safety? Oh the experience that I have had of the goodness of God, to me and mine!

THE SEVENTH REMOVE

After a restless and hungry night there, we had a wearisome time of it the next day. The swamp by which we lay was, as it were, a deep dungeon, and an exceeding high and steep hill before it. Before I got to the top of the hill, I thought my heart and legs, and all would have broken, and failed me. What, through faintness and soreness of body, it was a grievous day of travel to me. As we went along, I saw a place where English cattle had been. That was comfort to me, such as it was. Quickly after that we came to an English path, which so took with me, that I thought I could have freely lyen down and died. That day, a little after noon, we came to Squakeag, where the Indians quickly spread themselves over the deserted English fields, gleaning what they could find. Some picked up ears of wheat that were crickled down; some found ears of Indian corn; some found ground nuts, and others sheaves of wheat that were frozen together in the shock, and went to threshing of them out. Myself got two ears of Indian corn, and whilst I did but turn my back, one of them was stolen from me, which much troubled me. There came an Indian to them at that time with a basket of horse liver. I asked him to give me a piece. "What," says he, "can you eat horse liver?" I told him, I would try, if he would give a piece, which he did, and I laid it on the coals to roast. But before it was half ready they got half of it away from me, so that I was fain to take the rest and eat it as it was, with the blood about my mouth, and yet a savory bit it was to me: "For to the hungry soul every bitter thing is sweet." A solemn sight methought it was, to see fields of wheat and Indian corn forsaken and spoiled and the remainders of them to be food for our merciless enemies. That night we had a mess of wheat for our supper.

THE EIGHTH REMOVE

On the morrow morning we must go over the river, i.e. Connecticut, to meet with King Philip. Two canoes full they had carried over; the next turn I myself was to go. But as my foot was upon the canoe to step in there was a sudden outcry among them, and I must step back, and instead of going over the river, I must go four or five miles up the river farther northward. Some of the Indians ran one way, and some another. The cause of this rout was, as I thought, their espying some English scouts, who were thereabout. In this travel up the river about noon the company made a stop, and sat down; some to eat, and others to rest them. As I sat amongst them, musing of things past, my son Joseph unexpectedly came to me. We asked of each other's welfare, bemoaning our doleful condition, and the change that had come upon us. We had husband and father, and children, and sisters, and friends, and relations, and house, and home, and many comforts of this life: but now we may say, as Job, "Naked came I out of my mother's womb, and naked shall I return: the Lord gave, the Lord hath taken away, blessed be the name of the Lord." I asked him whether he would read. He told me he earnestly desired it, I gave him my Bible, and he lighted upon that comfortable Scripture "I shall not die but live, and declare the works of the Lord: the Lord hath chastened me sore yet he hath not given me over to death" (Psalm 118.17-18). "Look here, mother," says he, "did you read this?" And here I may take occasion to mention one principal ground of my setting forth these lines: even as the psalmist says, to declare the works of the Lord, and His wonderful power in carrying us along, preserving us in the wilderness, while under the enemy's hand, and returning of us in safety again. And His goodness in bringing to my hand so many comfortable and suitable scriptures in my distress. But to return, we traveled on till night; and in the morning, we must go over the river to Philip's crew. When I was in the canoe I could not but be amazed at the numerous crew of pagans that were on the bank on the other side. When I came ashore, they gathered all about me, I sitting alone in the midst. I observed they asked one another questions, and laughed, and rejoiced over their gains and victories. Then my heart began to fail: and I fell aweeping, which was the first time to my remembrance, that I wept before them. Although I had met with so much affliction, and my heart was many times ready to break, yet could I not shed one tear in their sight; but rather had been all this while in a maze, and like one astonished. But now I may say as Psalm 137.1, "By the Rivers of Babylon, there we sate down: yea, we wept when we remembered Zion." There one of them asked me why I wept. I could hardly tell what to say: Yet I answered, they would kill me. "No," said he, "none will hurt you." Then came one of them and gave me two spoonfuls of meal to comfort me, and another gave me half a pint of peas; which was more worth than many bushels at another time. Then I went to see King Philip. He bade me come in and sit down, and asked me whether I would smoke it (a usual compliment nowadays amongst saints and sinners) but this no way suited me. For though I had formerly used tobacco, yet I had left it ever since I was first taken. It seems to be a bait the devil lays to make men lose their precious time. I remember with shame how formerly, when I had taken two or three pipes, I was presently ready for another, such a bewitching thing it is. But I thank God, He has now given me power over it; surely there are many who may be better employed than to lie sucking a stinking tobacco-pipe.

Now the Indians gather their forces to go against Northampton. Over night one went about yelling and hooting to give notice of the design. Whereupon they fell to boiling of ground nuts, and parching of corn (as many as had it) for their provision; and in the morning away they went. During my abode in this place, Philip spake to me to make a shirt for his boy, which I did, for which he gave me a shilling. I offered the money to my master, but he bade me keep it; and with it I bought a piece of horse flesh. Afterwards he asked me to make a cap for his boy, for which he invited me to dinner. I went, and he gave me a pancake, about as big as two fingers. It was made of parched wheat, beaten, and fried in bear's grease, but I thought I never tasted pleasanter meat in my life. There was a squaw who spake to me to make a shirt for her sannup, for which she gave me a piece of bear. Another asked me to knit a pair of stockings, for which she gave me a quart of peas. I boiled my peas and bear together, and invited my master and mistress to dinner; but the proud gossip, because I served them both in one dish, would eat nothing, except one bit that he gave her upon the point of his knife. Hearing that my son was come to this place, I went to see him, and found him lying flat upon the ground. I asked him how he could sleep so? He answered me that he was not asleep, but at prayer; and lay so, that they might not observe what he was doing. I pray God he may remember these things now he is returned in safety. At this place (the sun now getting higher) what with the beams and heat of the sun, and the smoke of the wigwams, I thought I should have been blind. I could scarce discern one wigwam from another. There was here one Mary Thurston of Medfield, who seeing how it was with me, lent me a hat to wear; but as soon as I was gone, the squaw (who owned that Mary Thurston) came running after me, and got it away again. Here was the squaw that gave me one spoonful of meal. I put it in my pocket to keep it safe. Yet notwithstanding, somebody stole it, but put five Indian corns in the room of it; which corns were the greatest provisions I had in my travel for one day.

The Indians returning from Northampton, brought with them some horses, and sheep, and other things which they had taken; I desired them that they would carry me to Albany upon one of those horses, and sell me for powder: for so they had sometimes discoursed. I was utterly hopeless of getting home on foot, the way that I came. I could hardly bear to think of the many weary steps I had taken, to come to this place.

THE NINTH REMOVE

But instead of going either to Albany or homeward, we must go five miles up the river, and then go over it. Here we abode a while. Here lived a sorry Indian, who spoke to me to make him a shirt. When I had done it, he would pay me nothing. But he living by the riverside, where I often went to fetch water, I would often be putting of him in mind, and calling for my pay: At last he told me if I would make another shirt, for a papoose not yet born, he would give me a knife, which he did when I had done it. I carried the knife in, and my master asked me to give it him, and I was not a little glad that I had anything that they would accept of, and be pleased with. When we were at this place, my master's maid came home; she had been gone three weeks into the Narragansett country to fetch corn, where they had stored up some in the ground. She brought home about a peck and half of corn. This was about the time that their great captain, Naananto, was killed in the Narragansett country. My son being now about a mile from me, I asked liberty to go and see him; they bade me go, and away I went; but quickly lost myself, traveling over hills and through swamps, and could not find the way to him. And I cannot but admire at the wonderful power and goodness of God to me, in that, though I was gone from home, and met with all sorts of Indians, and those I had no knowledge of, and there being no Christian soul near me; yet not one of them offered the least imaginable miscarriage to me. I turned homeward again, and met with my master. He showed me the way to my son. When I came to him I found him not well: and withall he had a boil on his side, which much troubled him. We bemoaned one another a while, as the Lord helped us, and then I returned again. When I was returned, I found myself as unsatisfied as I was before. I went up and down mourning and lamenting; and my spirit was ready to sink with the thoughts of my poor children. My son was ill, and I could not but think of his mournful looks, and no Christian friend was near him, to do any office of love for him, either for soul or body. And my poor girl, I knew not where she was, nor whether she was sick, or well, or alive, or dead. I repaired under these thoughts to my Bible (my great comfort in that time) and that Scripture came to my hand, "Cast thy burden upon the Lord, and He shall sustain thee" (Psalm 55.22).

But I was fain to go and look after something to satisfy my hunger, and going among the wigwams, I went into one and there found a squaw who showed herself very kind to me, and gave me a piece of bear. I put it into my pocket, and came home, but could not find an opportunity to broil it, for fear they would get it from me, and there it lay all that day and night in my stinking pocket. In the morning I went to the same squaw, who had a kettle of ground nuts boiling. I asked her to let me boil my piece of bear in her kettle, which she did, and gave me some ground nuts to eat with it: and I cannot but think how pleasant it was to me. I have sometime seen bear baked very handsomely among the English, and some like it, but the thought that it was bear made me tremble. But now that was savory to me that one would think was enough to turn the stomach of a brute creature.

One bitter cold day I could find no room to sit down before the fire. I went out, and could not tell what to do, but I went in to another wigwam, where they were also sitting round the fire, but the squaw laid a skin for me, and bid me sit down, and gave me some ground nuts, and bade me come again; and told me they would buy me, if they were able, and yet these were strangers to me that I never saw before.

THE TENTH REMOVE

That day a small part of the company removed about three-quarters of a mile, intending further the next day. When they came to the place where they intended to lodge, and had pitched their wigwams, being hungry, I went again back to the place we were before at, to get something to eat, being encouraged by the squaw's kindness, who bade me come again. When I was there, there came an Indian to look after me, who when he had found me, kicked me all along. I went home and found venison roasting that night, but they would not give me one bit of it. Sometimes I met with favor, and sometimes with nothing but frowns.

THE ELEVENTH REMOVE

The next day in the morning they took their travel, intending a day's journey up the river. I took my load at my back, and quickly we came to wade over the river; and passed over tiresome and wearisome hills. One hill was so steep that I was fain to creep up upon my knees, and to hold by the twigs and bushes to keep myself from falling backward. My head also was so light that I usually reeled as I went; but I hope all these wearisome steps that I have taken, are but a forewarning to me of the heavenly rest: "I know, O Lord, that thy judgments are right, and that thou in faithfulness hast afflicted me" (Psalm 119.75).

THE TWELFTH REMOVE

It was upon a Sabbath-day-morning, that they prepared for their travel. This morning I asked my master whether he would sell me to my husband. He answered me "Nux," which did much rejoice my spirit. My mistress, before we went, was gone to the burial of a papoose, and returning, she found me sitting and reading in my Bible; she snatched it hastily out of my hand, and threw it out of doors. I ran out and catched it up, and put it into my pocket, and never let her see it afterward. Then they packed up their things to be gone, and gave me my load. I complained it was too heavy, whereupon she gave me a slap in the face, and bade me go; I lifted up my heart to God, hoping the redemption was not far off; and the rather because their insolency grew worse and worse.

But the thoughts of my going homeward (for so we bent our course) much cheered my spirit, and made my burden seem light, and almost nothing at all. But (to my amazement and great perplexity) the scale was soon turned; for when we had gone a little way, on a sudden my mistress gives out; she would go no further, but turn back again, and said I must go back again with her, and she called her sannup, and would have had him gone back also, but he would not, but said he would go on, and come to us again in three days. My spirit was, upon this, I confess, very impatient, and almost outrageous. I thought I could as well have died as went back; I cannot declare the trouble that I was in about it; but yet back again I must go. As soon as I had the opportunity, I took my Bible to read, and that quieting Scripture came to my hand, "Be still, and know that I am God" (Psalm 46.10). Which stilled my spirit for the present. But a sore time of trial, I concluded, I had to go through, my master being gone, who seemed to me the best friend that I had of an Indian, both in cold and hunger, and quickly so it proved. Down I sat, with my heart as full as it could hold, and yet so hungry that I could not sit neither; but going out to see what I could find, and walking among the trees, I found six acorns, and two chestnuts, which were some refreshment to me. Towards night I gathered some sticks for my own comfort, that I might not lie a-cold; but when we came to lie down they bade me to go out, and lie somewhere else, for they had company (they said) come in more than their own. I told them, I could not tell where to go, they bade me go look; I told them, if I went to another wigwam they would be angry, and send me home again. Then one of the company drew his sword, and told me he would run me through if I did not go presently. Then was I fain to stoop to this rude fellow, and to go out in the night, I knew not whither. Mine eyes have seen that fellow afterwards walking up and down Boston, under the appearance of a Friend Indian, and several others of the like cut. I went to one wigwam, and they told me they had no room. Then I went to another, and they said the same; at last an old Indian bade me to come to him, and his squaw gave me some ground nuts; she gave me also something to lay under my head, and a good fire we had; and through the good providence of God, I had a comfortable lodging that night. In the morning, another Indian bade me come at night, and he would give me six ground nuts, which I did. We were at this place and time about two miles from [the] Connecticut river. We went in the morning to gather ground nuts, to the river, and went back again that night. I went with a good load at my back (for they when they went, though but a little way, would carry all their trumpery with them). I told them the skin was off my back, but I had no other comforting answer from them than this: that it would be no matter if my head were off too.

THE THIRTEENTH REMOVE

Instead of going toward the Bay, which was that I desired, I must go with them five or six miles down the river into a mighty thicket of brush; where we abode almost a fortnight. Here one asked me to make a shirt for her papoose, for which she gave me a mess of broth, which was thickened with meal made of the bark of a tree, and to make it the better, she had put into it about a handful of peas, and a few roasted ground nuts. I had not seen my son a pretty while, and here was an Indian of whom I made inquiry after him, and asked him when he saw him. He answered me that such a time his master roasted him, and that himself did eat a piece of him, as big as his two fingers, and that he was very good meat. But the Lord upheld my Spirit, under this discouragement; and I considered their horrible addictedness to lying, and that there is not one of them that makes the least conscience of speaking of truth. In this place, on a cold night, as I lay by the fire, I removed a stick that kept the heat from me. A squaw moved it down again, at which I looked up, and she threw a handful of ashes in mine eyes. I thought I should have been quite blinded, and have never seen more, but lying down, the water run out of my eyes, and carried the dirt with it, that by the morning I recovered my sight again. Yet upon this, and the like occasions, I hope it is not too much to say with Job, "Have pity upon me, O ye my Friends, for the Hand of the Lord has touched me." And here I cannot but remember how many times sitting in their wigwams, and musing on things past, I should suddenly leap up and run out, as if I had been at home, forgetting where I was, and what my condition was; but when I was without, and saw nothing but wilderness, and woods, and a company of barbarous heathens, my mind quickly returned to me, which made me think of that, spoken concerning Sampson, who said, "I will go out and shake myself as at other times, but he wist not that the Lord was departed from him." About this time I began to think that all my hopes of restoration would come to nothing. I thought of the English army, and hoped for their coming, and being taken by them, but that failed. I hoped to be carried to Albany, as the Indians had discoursed before, but that failed also. I thought of being sold to my husband, as my master spake, but instead of that, my master himself was gone, and I left behind, so that my spirit was now quite ready to sink. I asked them to let me go out and pick up some sticks, that I might get alone, and pour out my heart unto the Lord. Then also I took my Bible to read, but I found no comfort here neither, which many times I was wont to find. So easy a thing it is with God to dry up the streams of Scripture comfort from us. Yet I can say, that in all my sorrows and afflictions, God did not leave me to have my impatience work towards Himself, as if His ways were unrighteous. But I knew that He laid upon me less than I deserved. Afterward, before this doleful time ended with me, I was turning the leaves of my Bible, and the Lord brought to me some Scriptures, which did a little revive me, as that [in] Isaiah 55.8: "For my thoughts are not your thoughts, neither are your ways my ways, saith the Lord." And also that [in] Psalm 37.5: "Commit thy way unto the Lord; trust also in him; and he shall bring it to pass." About this time they came yelping from Hadley, where they had killed three Englishmen, and brought one captive with them, viz. Thomas Read. They all gathered about the poor man, asking him many questions. I desired also to go and see him; and when I came, he was crying bitterly, supposing they would quickly kill him. Whereupon I asked one of them, whether they intended to kill him; he answered me, they would not. He being a little cheered with that, I asked him about the welfare of my husband. He told me he saw him such a time in the Bay, and he was well, but very melancholy. By which I certainly understood (though I suspected it before) that whatsoever the Indians told me respecting him was vanity and lies. Some of them told me he was dead, and they had killed him; some said he was married again, and that the Governor wished him to marry; and told him he should have his choice, and that all persuaded I was dead. So like were these barbarous creatures to him who was a liar from the beginning.

As I was sitting once in the wigwam here, Philip's maid came in with the child in her arms, and asked me to give her a piece of my apron, to make a flap for it. I told her I would not. Then my mistress bade me give it, but still I said no. The maid told me if I would not give her a piece, she would tear a piece off it. I told her I would tear her coat then. With that my mistress rises up, and take up a stick big enough to have killed me, and struck at me with it. But I stepped out, and she struck the stick into the mat of the wigwam. But while she was pulling of it out I ran to the maid and gave her all my apron, and so that storm went over.

Hearing that my son was come to this place, I went to see him, and told him his father was well, but melancholy. He told me he was as much grieved for his father as for himself. I wondered at his speech, for I thought I had enough upon my spirit in reference to myself, to make me mindless of my husband and everyone else; they being safe among their friends. He told me also, that awhile before, his master (together with other Indians) were going to the French for powder; but by the way the Mohawks met with them, and killed four of their company, which made the rest turn back again, for it might have been worse with him, had he been sold to the French, than it proved to be in his remaining with the Indians.

I went to see an English youth in this place, one John Gilbert of Springfield. I found him lying without doors, upon the ground. I asked him how he did? He told me he was very sick of a flux, with eating so much blood. They had turned him out of the wigwam, and with him an Indian papoose, almost dead (whose parents had been killed), in a bitter cold day, without fire or clothes. The young man himself had nothing on but his shirt and waistcoat. This sight was enough to melt a heart of flint. There they lay quivering in the cold, the youth round like a dog, the papoose stretched out with his eyes and nose and mouth full of dirt, and yet alive, and groaning. I advised John to go and get to some fire. He told me he could not stand, but I persuaded him still, lest he should lie there and die. And with much ado I got him to a fire, and went myself home. As soon as I was got home his master's daughter came after me, to know what I had done with the Englishman. I told her I had got him to a fire in such a place. Now had I need to pray Paul's Prayer "That we may be delivered from unreasonable and wicked men" (2 Thessalonians 3.2). For her satisfaction I went along with her, and brought her to him; but before I got home again it was noised about that I was running away and getting the English youth, along with me; that as soon as I came in they began to rant and domineer, asking me where I had been, and what I had been doing? and saying they would knock him on the head. I told them I had been seeing the English youth, and that I would not run away. They told me I lied, and taking up a hatchet, they came to me, and said they would knock me down if I stirred out again, and so confined me to the wigwam. Now may I say with David, "I am in a great strait" (2 Samuel 24.14). If I keep in, I must die with hunger, and if I go out, I must be knocked in head. This distressed condition held that day, and half the next. And then the Lord remembered me, whose mercies are great. Then came an Indian to me with a pair of stockings that were too big for him, and he would have me ravel them out, and knit them fit for him. I showed myself willing, and bid him ask my mistress if I might go along with him a little way; she said yes, I might, but I was not a little refreshed with that news, that I had my liberty again. Then I went along with him, and he gave me some roasted ground nuts, which did again revive my feeble stomach.

Being got out of her sight, I had time and liberty again to look into my Bible; which was my guide by day, and my pillow by night. Now that comfortable Scripture presented itself to me, "For a small moment have I forsaken thee, but with great mercies will I gather thee" (Isaiah 54.7). Thus the Lord carried me along from one time to another, and made good to me this precious promise, and many others. Then my son came to see me, and I asked his master to let him stay awhile with me, that I might comb his head, and look over him, for he was almost overcome with lice. He told me, when I had done, that he was very hungry, but I had nothing to relieve him, but bid him go into the wigwams as he went along, and see if he could get any thing among them. Which he did, and it seems tarried a little too long; for his master was angry with him, and beat him, and then sold him. Then he came running to tell me he had a new master, and that he had given him some ground nuts already. Then I went along with him to his new master who told me he loved him, and he should not want. So his master carried him away, and I never saw him afterward, till I saw him at Piscataqua in Portsmouth.

That night they bade me go out of the wigwam again. My mistress's papoose was sick, and it died that night, and there was one benefit in it—that there was more room. I went to a wigwam, and they bade me come in, and gave me a skin to lie upon, and a mess of venison and ground nuts, which was a choice dish among them. On the morrow they buried the papoose, and afterward, both morning and evening, there came a company to mourn and howl with her; though I confess I could not much condole with them. Many sorrowful days I had in this place, often getting alone. "Like a crane, or a swallow, so did I chatter; I did mourn as a dove, mine eyes ail with looking upward. Oh, Lord, I am oppressed; undertake for me" (Isaiah 38.14). I could tell the Lord, as Hezekiah, "Remember now O Lord, I beseech thee, how I have walked before thee in truth." Now had I time to examine all my ways: my conscience did not accuse me of unrighteousness toward one or other; yet I saw how in my walk with God, I had been a careless creature. As David said, "Against thee, thee only have I sinned": and I might say with the poor publican, "God be merciful unto me a sinner." On the Sabbath days, I could look upon the sun and think how people were going to the house of God, to have their souls refreshed; and then home, and their bodies also; but I was destitute of both; and might say as the poor prodigal, "He would fain have filled his belly with the husks that the swine did eat, and no man gave unto him" (Luke 15.16). For I must say with him, "Father, I have sinned against Heaven and in thy sight." I remembered how on the night before and after the Sabbath, when my family was about me, and relations and neighbors with us, we could pray and sing, and then refresh our bodies with the good creatures of God; and then have a comfortable bed to lie down on; but instead of all this, I had only a little swill for the body and then, like a swine, must lie down on the ground. I cannot express to man the sorrow that lay upon my spirit; the Lord knows it. Yet that comfortable Scripture would often come to mind, "For a small moment have I forsaken thee, but with great mercies will I gather thee."

THE FOURTEENTH REMOVE

Now must we pack up and be gone from this thicket, bending our course toward the Baytowns; I having nothing to eat by the way this day, but a few crumbs of cake, that an Indian gave my girl the same day we were taken. She gave it me, and I put it in my pocket; there it lay, till it was so moldy (for want of good baking) that one could not tell what it was made of; it fell all to crumbs, and grew so dry and hard, that it was like little flints; and this refreshed me many times, when I was ready to faint. It was in my thoughts when I put it into my mouth, that if ever I returned, I would tell the world what a blessing the Lord gave to such mean food. As we went along they killed a deer, with a young one in her, they gave me a piece of the fawn, and it was so young and tender, that one might eat the bones as well as the flesh, and yet I thought it very good. When night came on we sat down; it rained, but they quickly got up a bark wigwam, where I lay dry that night. I looked out in the morning, and many of them had lain in the rain all night, I saw by their reeking. Thus the Lord dealt mercifully with me many times, and I fared better than many of them. In the morning they took the blood of the deer, and put it into the paunch, and so boiled it. I could eat nothing of that, though they ate it sweetly. And yet they were so nice in other things, that when I had fetched water, and had put the dish I dipped the water with into the kettle of water which I brought, they would say they would knock me down; for they said, it was a sluttish trick.

THE FIFTEENTH REMOVE

We went on our travel. I having got one handful of ground nuts, for my support that day, they gave me my load, and I went on cheerfully (with the thoughts of going homeward), having my burden more on my back than my spirit. We came to Banquang river again that day, near which we abode a few days. Sometimes one of them would give me a pipe, another a little tobacco, another a little salt: which I would change for a little victuals. I cannot but think what a wolvish appetite persons have in a starving condition; for many times when they gave me that which was hot, I was so greedy, that I should burn my mouth, that it would trouble me hours after, and yet I should quickly do the same again. And after I was thoroughly hungry, I was never again satisfied. For though sometimes it fell out, that I got enough, and did eat till I could eat no more, yet I was as unsatisfied as I was when I began. And now could I see that Scripture verified (there being many Scriptures which we do not take notice of, or understand till we are afflicted) "Thou shalt eat and not be satisfied" (Micah 6.14). Now might I see more than ever before, the miseries that sin hath brought upon us. Many times I should be ready to run against the heathen, but the Scripture would quiet me again, "Shall there be evil in a City and the Lord hath not done it?" (Amos 3.6). The Lord help me to make a right improvement of His word, and that I might learn that great lesson: "He hath showed thee (Oh Man) what is good, and what doth the Lord require of thee, but to do justly, and love mercy, and walk humbly with thy God? Hear ye the rod, and who hath appointed it" (Micah 6.8-9).

THE SIXTEENTH REMOVAL

We began this remove with wading over Banquang river: the water was up to the knees, and the stream very swift, and so cold that I thought it would have cut me in sunder. I was so weak and feeble, that I reeled as I went along, and thought there I must end my days at last, after my bearing and getting through so many difficulties. The Indians stood laughing to see me staggering along; but in my distress the Lord gave me experience of the truth, and goodness of that promise, "When thou passest through the waters, I will be with thee; and through the rivers, they shall not overflow thee" (Isaiah 43.2). Then I sat down to put on my stockings and shoes, with the tears running down mine eyes, and sorrowful thoughts in my heart, but I got up to go along with them. Quickly there came up to us an Indian, who informed them that I must go to Wachusett to my master, for there was a letter come from the council to the Sagamores, about redeeming the captives, and that there would be another in fourteen days, and that I must be there ready. My heart was so heavy before that I could scarce speak or go in the path; and yet now so light, that I could run. My strength seemed to come again, and recruit my feeble knees, and aching heart. Yet it pleased them to go but one mile that night, and there we stayed two days. In that time came a company of Indians to us, near thirty, all on horseback. My heart skipped within me, thinking they had been Englishmen at the first sight of them, for they were dressed in English apparel, with hats, white neckcloths, and sashes about their waists; and ribbons upon their shoulders; but when they came near, there was a vast difference between the lovely faces of Christians, and foul looks of those heathens, which much damped my spirit again.

THE SEVENTEENTH REMOVE

A comfortable remove it was to me, because of my hopes. They gave me a pack, and along we went cheerfully; but quickly my will proved more than my strength; having little or no refreshing, my strength failed me, and my spirits were almost quite gone. Now may I say with David "I am poor and needy, and my heart is wounded within me. I am gone like the shadow when it declineth: I am tossed up and down like the locust; my knees are weak through fasting, and my flesh faileth of fatness" (Psalm 119.22-24). At night we came to an Indian town, and the Indians sat down by a wigwam discoursing, but I was almost spent, and could scarce speak. I laid down my load, and went into the wigwam, and there sat an Indian boiling of horses feet (they being wont to eat the flesh first, and when the feet were old and dried, and they had nothing else, they would cut off the feet and use them). I asked him to give me a little of his broth, or water they were boiling in; he took a dish, and gave me one spoonful of samp, and bid me take as much of the broth as I would. Then I put some of the hot water to the samp, and drank it up, and my spirit came again. He gave me also a piece of the ruff or ridding of the small guts, and I broiled it on the coals; and now may I say with Jonathan, "See, I pray you, how mine eyes have been enlightened, because I tasted a little of this honey" (1 Samuel 14.29). Now is my spirit revived again; though means be never so inconsiderable, yet if the Lord bestow His blessing upon them, they shall refresh both soul and body.

THE EIGHTEENTH REMOVE

We took up our packs and along we went, but a wearisome day I had of it. As we went along I saw an Englishman stripped naked, and lying dead upon the ground, but knew not who it was. Then we came to another Indian town, where we stayed all night. In this town there were four English children, captives; and one of them my own sister's. I went to see how she did, and she was well, considering her captive condition. I would have tarried that night with her, but they that owned her would not suffer it. Then I went into another wigwam, where they were boiling corn and beans, which was a lovely sight to see, but I could not get a taste thereof. Then I went to another wigwam, where there were two of the English children; the squaw was boiling horses feet; then she cut me off a little piece, and gave one of the English children a piece also. Being very hungry I had quickly eat up mine, but the child could not bite it, it was so tough and sinewy, but lay sucking, gnawing, chewing and slab-bering of it in the mouth and hand. Then I took it of the child, and eat it myself, and savory it was to my taste. Then I may say as Job 6.7, "The things that my soul refused to touch are as my sorrowful meat." Thus the Lord made that pleasant refreshing, which another time would have been an abomination. Then I went home to my mistress's wigwam; and they told me I disgraced my master with begging, and if I did so any more, they would knock me in the head. I told them, they had as good knock me in head as starve me to death.

THE NINETEENTH REMOVE

They said, when we went out, that we must travel to Wa-chusett this day. But a bitter weary day I had of it, traveling now three days together, without resting any day between. At last, after many weary steps, I saw Wachusett hills, but many miles off. Then we came to a great swamp, through which we traveled, up to the knees in mud and water, which was heavy going to one tired before. Being almost spent, I thought I should have sunk down at last, and never got out; but I may say, as in Psalm 94.18, "When my foot slipped, thy mercy, O Lord, held me up." Going along, having indeed my life, but little spirit, Philip, who was in the company, came up and took me by the hand, and said, two weeks more and you shall be mistress again. I asked him, if he spake true? He answered, "Yes, and quickly you shall come to your master again; who had been gone from us three weeks." After many weary steps we came to Wachusett, where he was: and glad I was to see him. He asked me, when I washed me? I told him not this month. Then he fetched me some water himself, and bid me wash, and gave me the glass to see how I looked; and bid his squaw give me something to eat. So she gave me a mess of beans and meat, and a little ground nut cake. I was wonder-fully revived with this favor showed me: "He made them also to be pitied of all those that carried them captives" (Psalm 106.46).

My master had three squaws, living sometimes with one, and sometimes with another one, this old squaw, at whose wig-wam I was, and with whom my master had been those three weeks. Another was Wattimore [Weetamoo] with whom I had lived and served all this while. A severe and proud dame she was, bestowing every day in dressing herself neat as much time as any of the gentry of the land: powdering her hair, and paint-ing her face, going with necklaces, with jewels in her ears, and bracelets upon her hands. When she had dressed herself, her work was to make girdles of wampum and beads. The third squaw was a younger one, by whom he had two papooses. By the time I was refreshed by the old squaw, with whom my master was, Weetamoo's maid came to call me home, at which I fell aweeping. Then the old squaw told me, to encourage me, that if I wanted victuals, I should come to her, and that I should lie there in her wigwam. Then I went with the maid, and quickly came again and lodged there. The squaw laid a mat under me, and a good rug over me; the first time I had any such kindness showed me. I understood that Weetamoo thought that if she should let me go and serve with the old squaw, she would be in danger to lose not only my service, but the redemption pay also. And I was not a little glad to hear this; being by it raised in my hopes, that in God's due time there would be an end of this sorrowful hour. Then came an Indian, and asked me to knit him three pair of stockings, for which I had a hat, and a silk handkerchief. Then another asked me to make her a shift, for which she gave me an apron.

Then came Tom and Peter, with the second letter from the council, about the captives. Though they were Indians, I got them by the hand, and burst out into tears. My heart was so full that I could not speak to them; but recovering myself, I asked them how my husband did, and all my friends and acquaintance? They said, "They are all very well but melancholy." They brought me two biscuits, and a pound of tobacco. The tobacco I quickly gave away. When it was all gone, one asked me to give him a pipe of tobacco. I told him it was all gone. Then began he to rant and threaten. I told him when my husband came I would give him some. Hang him rogue (says he) I will knock out his brains, if he comes here. And then again, in the same breath they would say that if there should come an hundred without guns, they would do them no hurt. So unstable and like madmen they were. So that fearing the worst, I durst not send to my husband, though there were some thoughts of his coming to redeem and fetch me, not knowing what might follow. For there was little more trust to them than to the master they served. When the letter was come, the Sagamores met to consult about the captives, and called me to them to inquire how much my husband would give to redeem me. When I came I sat down among them, as I was wont to do, as their manner is. Then they bade me stand up, and said they were the General Court. They bid me speak what I thought he would give. Now knowing that all we had was destroyed by the Indians, I was in a great strait. I thought if I should speak of but a little it would be slighted, and hinder the matter; if of a great sum, I knew not where it would be procured. Yet at a venture I said "Twenty pounds," yet desired them to take less. But they would not hear of that, but sent that message to Boston, that for twenty pounds I should be redeemed. It was a Praying Indian that wrote their letter for them. There was another Praying Indian, who told me, that he had a brother, that would not eat horse; his conscience was so tender and scrupulous (though as large as hell, for the destruction of poor Christians). Then he said, he read that Scripture to him, "There was a famine in Samaria, and behold they besieged it, until an ass's head was sold for four-score pieces of silver, and the fourth part of a cab of dove's dung for five pieces of silver" (2 Kings 6.25). He expounded this place to his brother, and showed him that it was lawful to eat that in a famine which is not at another time. And now, says he, he will eat horse with any Indian of them all. There was another Praying Indian, who when he had done all the mischief that he could, betrayed his own father into the English hands, thereby to purchase his own life. Another Praying Indian was at Sudbury fight, though, as he deserved, he was afterward hanged for it. There was another Praying Indian, so wicked and cruel, as to wear a string about his neck, strung with Christians' fingers. Another Praying Indian, when they went to Sudbury fight, went with them, and his squaw also with him, with her papoose at her back. Before they went to that fight they got a company together to pow-wow. The manner was as followeth: there was one that kneeled upon a deerskin, with the company round him in a ring who kneeled, and striking upon the ground with their hands, and with sticks, and muttering or humming with their mouths. Besides him who kneeled in the ring, there also stood one with a gun in his hand. Then he on the deerskin made a speech, and all manifested assent to it; and so they did many times together. Then they bade him with the gun go out of the ring, which he did. But when he was out, they called him in again; but he seemed to make a stand; then they called the more earnestly, till he returned again. Then they all sang. Then they gave him two guns, in either hand one. And so he on the deerskin began again; and at the end of every sentence in his speaking, they all assented, humming or muttering with their mouths, and striking upon the ground with their hands. Then they bade him with the two guns go out of the ring again; which he did, a little way. Then they called him in again, but he made a stand. So they called him with greater earnestness; but he stood reeling and wavering as if he knew not whither he should stand or fall, or which way to go. Then they called him with exceeding great vehemency, all of them, one and another. After a little while he turned in, staggering as he went, with his arms stretched out, in either hand a gun. As soon as he came in they all sang and rejoiced exceedingly a while. And then he upon the deerskin, made another speech unto which they all assented in a rejoicing manner. And so they ended their business, and forthwith went to Sudbury fight. To my thinking they went without any scruple, but that they should prosper, and gain the victory. And they went out not so rejoicing, but they came home with as great a victory. For they said they had killed two captains and almost an hundred men. One Englishman they brought along with them: and he said, it was too true, for they had made sad work at Sudbury, as indeed it proved. Yet they came home without that rejoicing and triumphing over their victory which they were wont to show at other times; but rather like dogs (as they say) which have lost their ears. Yet I could not perceive that it was for their own loss of men. They said they had not lost above five or six; and I missed none, except in one wigwam. When they went, they acted as if the devil had told them that they should gain the victory; and now they acted as if the devil had told them they should have a fall. Whither it were so or no, I cannot tell, but so it proved, for quickly they began to fall, and so held on that summer, till they came to utter ruin. They came home on a Sabbath day, and the Powaw that kneeled upon the deer-skin came home (I may say, without abuse) as black as the devil. When my master came home, he came to me and bid me make a shirt for his papoose, of a holland-laced pillowbere. About that time there came an Indian to me and bid me come to his wigwam at night, and he would give me some pork and ground nuts. Which I did, and as I was eating, another Indian said to me, he seems to be your good friend, but he killed two Englishmen at Sudbury, and there lie their clothes behind you: I looked behind me, and there I saw bloody clothes, with bullet-holes in them. Yet the Lord suffered not this wretch to do me any hurt. Yea, instead of that, he many times refreshed me; five or six times did he and his squaw refresh my feeble carcass. If I went to their wigwam at any time, they would always give me something, and yet they were strangers that I never saw before. Another squaw gave me a piece of fresh pork, and a little salt with it, and lent me her pan to fry it in; and I cannot but remember what a sweet, pleasant and delightful relish that bit had to me, to this day. So little do we prize common mercies when we have them to the full.

THE TWENTIETH REMOVE

It was their usual manner to remove, when they had done any mischief, lest they should be found out; and so they did at this time. We went about three or four miles, and there they built a great wigwam, big enough to hold an hundred Indians, which they did in preparation to a great day of dancing. They would say now amongst themselves, that the governor would be so angry for his loss at Sudbury, that he would send no more about the captives, which made me grieve and tremble. My sister being not far from the place where we now were, and hearing that I was here, desired her master to let her come and see me, and he was willing to it, and would go with her; but she being ready before him, told him she would go before, and was come within a mile or two of the place. Then he overtook her, and began to rant as if he had been mad, and made her go back again in the rain; so that I never saw her till I saw her in Charlestown.

But the Lord requited many of their ill doings, for this Indian her master, was hanged afterward at Boston. The Indians now began to come from all quarters, against their merry dancing day. Among some of them came one goodwife Kettle. I told her my heart was so heavy that it was ready to break. "So is mine too," said she, but yet said, "I hope we shall hear some good news shortly." I could hear how earnestly my sister desired to see me, and I as earnestly desired to see her; and yet neither of us could get an opportunity. My daughter was also now about a mile off, and I had not seen her in nine or ten weeks, as I had not seen my sister since our first taking. I earnestly desired them to let me go and see them: yea, I entreated, begged, and persuaded them, but to let me see my daughter; and yet so hard-hearted were they, that they would not suffer it. They made use of their tyrannical power whilst they had it; but through the Lord's wonderful mercy, their time was now but short.

On a Sabbath day, the sun being about an hour high in the afternoon, came Mr. John Hoar (the council permitting him, and his own foreward spirit inclining him), together with the two forementioned Indians, Tom and Peter, with their third letter from the council. When they came near, I was abroad. Though I saw them not, they presently called me in, and bade me sit down and not stir. Then they catched up their guns, and away they ran, as if an enemy had been at hand, and the guns went off apace. I manifested some great trouble, and they asked me what was the matter? I told them I thought they had killed the Englishman (for they had in the meantime informed me that an Englishman was come). They said, no. They shot over his horse and under and before his horse, and they pushed him this way and that way, at their pleasure, showing what they could do. Then they let them come to their wigwams. I begged of them to let me see the Englishman, but they would not. But there was I fain to sit their pleasure. When they had talked their fill with him, they suffered me to go to him. We asked each other of our welfare, and how my husband did, and all my friends? He told me they were all well, and would be glad to see me. Amongst other things which my husband sent me, there came a pound of tobacco, which I sold for nine shillings in money; for many of the

Indians for want of tobacco, smoked hemlock, and ground ivy. It was a great mistake in any, who thought I sent for tobacco; for through the favor of God, that desire was overcome. I now asked them whether I should go home with Mr. Hoar? They answered no, one and another of them, and it being night, we lay down with that answer. In the morning Mr. Hoar invited the Sagamores to dinner; but when we went to get it ready we found that they had stolen the greatest part of the provision Mr. Hoar had brought, out of his bags, in the night. And we may see the wonderful power of God, in that one passage, in that when there was such a great number of the Indians together, and so greedy of a little good food, and no English there but Mr. Hoar and myself, that there they did not knock us in the head, and take what we had, there being not only some provision, but also trading-cloth, a part of the twenty pounds agreed upon. But instead of doing us any mischief, they seemed to be ashamed of the fact, and said, it were some matchit Indian that did it. Oh, that we could believe that there is nothing too hard for God! God showed His power over the heathen in this, as He did over the hungry lions when Daniel was cast into the den. Mr. Hoar called them betime to dinner, but they ate very little, they being so busy in dressing themselves, and getting ready for their dance, which was carried on by eight of them, four men and four squaws. My master and mistress being two. He was dressed in his holland shirt, with great laces sewed at the tail of it; he had his silver buttons, his white stockings, his garters were hung round with shillings, and he had girdles of wampum upon his head and shoulders. She had a kersey coat, and covered with girdles of wampum from the loins upward. Her arms from her elbows to her hands were covered with bracelets; there were handfuls of necklaces about her neck, and several sorts of jewels in her ears. She had fine red stockings, and white shoes, her hair powdered and face painted red, that was always before black. And all the dancers were after the same manner. There were two others singing and knocking on a kettle for their music. They kept hopping up and down one after another, with a kettle of water in the midst, standing warm upon some embers, to drink of when they were dry. They held on till it was almost night, throwing out wampum to the standers by. At night I asked them again, if I should go home? They all as one said no, except my husband would come for me. When we were lain down, my master went out of the wigwam, and by and by sent in an Indian called James the Printer, who told Mr. Hoar, that my master would let me go home tomorrow, if he would let him have one pint of liquors. Then Mr. Hoar called his own Indians, Tom and Peter, and bid them go and see whether he would promise it before them three; and if he would, he should have it; which he did, and he had it. Then Philip smelling the business called me to him, and asked me what I would give him, to tell me some good news, and speak a good word for me. I told him I could not tell what to give him. I would [give him] anything I had, and asked him what he would have? He said two coats and twenty shillings in money, and half a bushel of seed corn, and some tobacco. I thanked him for his love; but I knew the good news as well as the crafty fox. My master after he had had his drink, quickly came ranting into the wigwam again, and called for Mr. Hoar, drinking to him, and saying, he was a good man, and then again he would say, "hang him rogue." Being almost drunk, he would drink to him, and yet presently say he should be hanged. Then he called for me. I trembled to hear him, yet I was fain to go to him, and he drank to me, showing no incivility. He was the first Indian I saw drunk all the while that I was amongst them. At last his squaw ran out, and he after her, round the wigwam, with his money jingling at his knees. But she escaped him. But having an old squaw he ran to her; and so through the Lord's mercy, we were no more troubled that night. Yet I had not a comfortable night's rest; for I think I can say, I did not sleep for three nights together. The night before the letter came from the council, I could not rest, I was so full of fears and troubles, God many times leaving us most in the dark, when deliverance is nearest. Yea, at this time I could not rest night nor day. The next night I was overjoyed, Mr. Hoar being come, and that with such good tidings. The third night I was even swallowed up with the thoughts of things, viz. that ever I should go home again; and that I must go, leaving my children behind me in the wilderness; so that sleep was now almost departed from mine eyes.

On Tuesday morning they called their general court (as they call it) to consult and determine, whether I should go home or no. And they all as one man did seemingly consent to it, that I should go home; except Philip, who would not come among them.

But before I go any further, I would take leave to mention a few remarkable passages of providence, which I took special notice of in my afflicted time.

1. Of the fair opportunity lost in the long march, a little after the fort fight, when our English army was so numerous, and in pursuit of the enemy, and so near as to take several and destroy them, and the enemy in such distress for food that our men might track them by their rooting in the earth for ground nuts, whilst they were flying for their lives. I say, that then our army should want provision, and be forced to leave their pursuit and return homeward; and the very next week the enemy came upon our town, like bears bereft of their whelps, or so many ravenous wolves, rending us and our lambs to death. But what shall I say? God seemed to leave his People to themselves, and order all things for His own holy ends. Shall there be evil in the City and the Lord hath not done it? They are not grieved for the affliction of Joseph, therefore shall they go captive, with the first that go captive. It is the Lord's doing, and it should be marvelous in our eyes.

2. I cannot but remember how the Indians derided the slowness, and dullness of the English army, in its setting out. For after the desolations at Lancaster and Medfield, as I went along with them, they asked me when I thought the English army would come after them? I told them I could not tell. "It may be they will come in May," said they. Thus did they scoff at us, as if the English would be a quarter of a year getting ready.

3. Which also I have hinted before, when the English army with new supplies were sent forth to pursue after the enemy, and they understanding it, fled before them till they came to Banquang river, where they forthwith went over safely; that that river should be impassable to the English. I can but admire to see the wonderful providence of God in preserving the heathen

for further affliction to our poor country. They could go in great numbers over, but the English must stop. God had an over-ruling hand in all those things.

4. It was thought, if their corn were cut down, they would starve and die with hunger, and all their corn that could be found, was destroyed, and they driven from that little they had in store, into the woods in the midst of winter; and yet how to admiration did the Lord preserve them for His holy ends, and the destruction of many still amongst the English! strangely did the Lord provide for them; that I did not see (all the time I was among them) one man, woman, or child, die with hunger.

Though many times they would eat that, that a hog or a dog would hardly touch; yet by that God strengthened them to be a scourge to His people.

The chief and commonest food was ground nuts. They eat also nuts and acorns, artichokes, lilly roots, ground beans, and several other weeds and roots, that I know not.

They would pick up old bones, and cut them to pieces at the joints, and if they were full of worms and maggots, they would scald them over the fire to make the vermine come out, and then boil them, and drink up the liquor, and then beat the great ends of them in a mortar, and so eat them. They would eat horse's guts, and ears, and all sorts of wild birds which they could catch; also bear, venison, beaver, tortoise, frogs, squirrels, dogs, skunks, rattlesnakes; yea, the very bark of trees; besides all sorts of creatures, and provision which they plundered from the English. I can but stand in admiration to see the wonderful power of God in providing for such a vast number of our ene-mies in the wilderness, where there was nothing to be seen, but from hand to mouth. Many times in a morning, the generality of them would eat up all they had, and yet have some further sup-ply against they wanted. It is said, "Oh, that my People had hearkened to me, and Israel had walked in my ways, I should soon have subdued their Enemies, and turned my hand against their Adversaries" (Psalm 81.13-14). But now our perverse and evil carriages in the sight of the Lord, have so offended Him, that instead of turning His hand against them, the Lord feeds and nourishes them up to be a scourge to the whole land.

5. Another thing that I would observe is the strange providence of God, in turning things about when the Indians was at the highest, and the English at the lowest. I was with the enemy eleven weeks and five days, and not one week passed without the fury of the enemy, and some desolation by fire and sword upon one place or other. They mourned (with their black faces) for their own losses, yet triumphed and rejoiced in their inhumane, and many times devilish cruelty to the English. They would boast much of their victories; saying that in two hours time they had destroyed such a captain and his company at such a place; and boast how many towns they had destroyed, and then scoff, and say they had done them a good turn to send them to Heaven so soon. Again, they would say this summer that they would knock all the rogues in the head, or drive them into the sea, or make them fly the country; thinking surely, Agag-like, "The bitterness of Death is past." Now the heathen begins to think all is their own, and the poor Christians' hopes to fail (as to man) and now their eyes are more to God, and their hearts sigh heaven-ward; and to say in good earnest, "Help Lord, or we perish." When the Lord had brought His people to this, that they saw no help in anything but Himself; then He takes the quarrel into His own hand; and though they had made a pit, in their own imaginations, as deep as hell for the Christians that summer, yet the Lord hurled themselves into it. And the Lord had not so many ways before to preserve them, but now He hath as many to destroy them.

But to return again to my going home, where we may see a remarkable change of providence. At first they were all against it, except my husband would come for me, but afterwards they assented to it, and seemed much to rejoice in it; some asked me to send them some bread, others some tobacco, others shaking me by the hand, offering me a hood and scarfe to ride in; not one moving hand or tongue against it. Thus hath the Lord answered my poor desire, and the many earnest requests of others put up unto God for me. In my travels an Indian came to me and told me, if I were willing, he and his squaw would run away, and go home along with me. I told him no: I was not willing to run away, but desired to wait God's time, that I might go home quietly, and without fear. And now God hath granted me my desire. O the wonderful power of God that I have seen, and the experience that I have had. I have been in the midst of those roaring lions, and savage bears, that feared neither God, nor man, nor the devil, by night and day, alone and in company, sleeping all sorts together, and yet not one of them ever offered me the least abuse of unchastity to me, in word or action. Though some are ready to say I speak it for my own credit; but I speak it in the presence of God, and to His Glory. God's power is as great now, and as sufficient to save, as when He preserved Daniel in the lion's den; or the three children in the fiery furnace. I may well say as his Psalm 107.12 "Oh give thanks unto the Lord for he is good, for his mercy endureth for ever." Let the redeemed of the Lord say so, whom He hath redeemed from the hand of the enemy, especially that I should come away in the midst of so many hundreds of enemies quietly and peaceably, and not a dog moving his tongue. So I took my leave of them, and in coming along my heart melted into tears, more than all the while I was with them, and I was almost swallowed up with the thoughts that ever I should go home again. About the sun going down, Mr. Hoar, and myself, and the two Indians came to Lancaster, and a solemn sight it was to me. There had I lived many comfortable years amongst my relations and neighbors, and now not one Christian to be seen, nor one house left standing. We went on to a farmhouse that was yet standing, where we lay all night, and a comfortable lodging we had, though nothing but straw to lie on. The Lord preserved us in safety that night, and raised us up again in the morning, and carried us along, that before noon, we came to Concord. Now was I full of joy, and yet not without sorrow; joy to see such a lovely sight, so many Christians together, and some of them my neighbors. There I met with my brother, and my brother-in-law, who asked me, if I knew where his wife was? Poor heart! he had helped to bury her, and knew it not. She being shot down by the house was partly burnt, so that those who were at Boston at the desolation of the town, and came back afterward, and buried the dead, did not know her. Yet I was not without sorrow, to think how many were looking and longing, and my own children amongst the rest, to enjoy that deliverance that I had now received, and I did not know whether ever I should see them again. Being recruited with food and raiment we went to Boston that day, where I met with my dear husband, but the thoughts of our dear children, one being dead, and the other we could not tell where, abated our comfort each to other. I was not before so much hemmed in with the merciless and cruel heathen, but now as much with pitiful, ten- der-hearted and compassionate Christians. In that poor, and distressed, and beggarly condition I was received in; I was kindly entertained in several houses. So much love I received from several (some of whom I knew, and others I knew not) that I am not capable to declare it. But the Lord knows them all by name. The Lord reward them sevenfold into their bosoms of His spirituals, for their temporals. The twenty pounds, the price of my redemption, was raised by some Boston gentlemen, and Mrs. Usher, whose bounty and religious charity, I would not forget to make mention of. Then Mr. Thomas Shepard of Charlestown received us into his house, where we continued eleven weeks; and a father and mother they were to us. And many more ten- der-hearted friends we met with in that place. We were now in the midst of love, yet not without much and frequent heaviness of heart for our poor children, and other relations, who were still in affliction. The week following, after my coming in, the gover- nor and council sent forth to the Indians again; and that not without success; for they brought in my sister, and goodwife Kettle. Their not knowing where our children were was a sore trial to us still, and yet we were not without secret hopes that we should see them again. That which was dead lay heavier upon my spirit, than those which were alive and amongst the heathen: thinking how it suffered with its wounds, and I was no way able to relieve it; and how it was buried by the heathen in the wilderness from among all Christians. We were hurried up and down in our thoughts, sometime we should hear a report that they were gone this way, and sometimes that; and that they were come in, in this place or that. We kept inquiring and listening to hear concerning them, but no certain news as yet. About this time the council had ordered a day of public thanks-giving. Though I thought I had still cause of mourning, and being unsettled in our minds, we thought we would ride toward the eastward, to see if we could hear anything concerning our children. And as we were riding along (God is the wise disposer of all things) between Ipswich and Rowley we met with Mr. William Hubbard, who told us that our son Joseph was come in to Major Waldron's, and another with him, which was my sis-ter's son. I asked him how he knew it? He said the major himself told him so. So along we went till we came to Newbury; and their minister being absent, they desired my husband to preach the thanksgiving for them; but he was not willing to stay there that night, but would go over to Salisbury, to hear further, and come again in the morning, which he did, and preached there that day. At night, when he had done, one came and told him that his daughter was come in at Providence. Here was mercy on both hands. Now hath God fulfilled that precious Scripture which was such a comfort to me in my distressed condition. When my heart was ready to sink into the earth (my children being gone, I could not tell whither) and my knees trembling under me, and I was walking through the valley of the shadow of death; then the Lord brought, and now has fulfilled that reviving word unto me: "Thus saith the Lord, Refrain thy voice from weeping, and thine eyes from tears, for thy Work shall be re-warded, saith the Lord, and they shall come again from the Land of the Enemy." Now we were between them, the one on the east, and the other on the west. Our son being nearest, we went to him first, to Portsmouth, where we met with him, and with the Major also, who told us he had done what he could, but could not redeem him under seven pounds, which the good people thereabouts were pleased to pay. The Lord reward the major, and all the rest, though unknown to me, for their labor of Love. My sister's son was redeemed for four pounds, which the coun-cil gave order for the payment of. Having now received one of our children, we hastened toward the other. Going back through Newbury my husband preached there on the Sabbath day; for which they rewarded him many fold.

On Monday we came to Charlestown, where we heard that the governor of Rhode Island had sent over for our daughter, to take care of her, being now within his jurisdiction; which should not pass without our acknowledgments. But she being nearer Rehoboth than Rhode Island, Mr. Newman went over, and took care of her and brought her to his own house. And the goodness of God was admirable to us in our low estate, in that He raised up passionate friends on every side to us, when we had nothing to recompense any for their love. The Indians were now gone that way, that it was apprehended dangerous to go to her. But the carts which carried provision to the English army, being guarded, brought her with them to Dorchester, where we received her safe. Blessed be the Lord for it, for great is His power, and He can do whatsoever seemeth Him good. Her coming in was after this manner: she was traveling one day with the Indians, with her basket at her back; the company of Indians were got before her, and gone out of sight, all except one squaw; she followed the squaw till night, and then both of them lay down, having nothing over them but the heavens and under them but the earth. Thus she traveled three days together, not knowing whither she was going; having nothing to eat or drink but water, and green hirtle-berries. At last they came into Providence, where she was kindly entertained by several of that town. The Indians often said that I should never have her under twenty pounds. But now the Lord hath brought her in upon free-cost, and given her to me the second time. The Lord make us a blessing indeed, each to others. Now have I seen that Scripture also fulfilled, "If any of thine be driven out to the outmost parts of heaven, from thence will the Lord thy God gather thee, and from thence will he fetch thee. And the Lord thy God will put all these curses upon thine enemies, and on them which hate thee, which persecuted thee" (Deuteronomy 30.4-7). Thus hath the Lord brought me and mine out of that horrible pit, and hath set us in the midst of tender-hearted and compassionate Christians. It is the desire of my soul that we may walk worthy of the mercies received, and which we are receiving.

Our family being now gathered together (those of us that were living), the South Church in Boston hired an house for us.

Then we removed from Mr. Shepard's, those cordial friends, and went to Boston, where we continued about three-quarters of a year. Still the Lord went along with us, and provided graciously for us. I thought it somewhat strange to set up house-keeping with bare walls; but as Solomon says, "Money answers all things" and that we had through the benevolence of Christian friends, some in this town, and some in that, and others; and some from England; that in a little time we might look, and see the house furnished with love. The Lord hath been exceeding good to us in our low estate, in that when we had neither house nor home, nor other necessaries, the Lord so moved the hearts of these and those towards us, that we wanted neither food, nor raiment for ourselves or ours: "There is a Friend which sticketh closer than a Brother" (Proverbs 18.24). And how many such friends have we found, and now living amongst? And truly such a friend have we found him to be unto us, in whose house we lived, viz. Mr. James Whitcomb, a friend unto us near hand, and afar off.

I can remember the time when I used to sleep quietly without workings in my thoughts, whole nights together, but now it is other ways with me. When all are fast about me, and no eye open, but His who ever waketh, my thoughts are upon things past, upon the awful dispensation of the Lord towards us, upon His wonderful power and might, in carrying of us through so many difficulties, in returning us in safety, and suffering none to hurt us. I remember in the night season, how the other day I was in the midst of thousands of enemies, and nothing but death before me. It is then hard work to persuade myself, that ever I should be satisfied with bread again. But now we are fed with the finest of the wheat, and, as I may say, with honey out of the rock. Instead of the husk, we have the fatted calf. The thoughts of these things in the particulars of them, and of the love and goodness of God towards us, make it true of me, what David said of himself, "I watered my Couch with my tears" (Psalm 6.6). Oh! the wonderful power of God that mine eyes have seen, affording matter enough for my thoughts to run in, that when others are sleeping mine eyes are weeping.

I have seen the extreme vanity of this world: One hour I have been in health, and wealthy, wanting nothing. But the next hour in sickness and wounds, and death, having nothing but sorrow and affliction.

Before I knew what affliction meant, I was ready sometimes to wish for it. When I lived in prosperity, having the comforts of the world about me, my relations by me, my heart cheerful, and taking little care for anything, and yet seeing many, whom I preferred before myself, under many trials and afflictions, in sickness, weakness, poverty, losses, crosses, and cares of the world, I should be sometimes jealous least I should have my portion in this life, and that Scripture would come to my mind, "For whom the Lord loveth he chasteneth, and scourgeth every Son whom he receiveth" (Hebrews 12.6). But now I see the Lord had His time to scourge and chasten me. The portion of some is to have their afflictions by drops, now one drop and then another; but the dregs of the cup, the wine of astonishment, like a sweeping rain that leaveth no food, did the Lord prepare to be my portion. Affliction I wanted, and affliction I had, full measure (I thought), pressed down and running over. Yet I see, when God calls a person to anything, and through never so many difficulties, yet He is fully able to carry them through and make them see, and say they have been gainers thereby. And I hope I can say in some measure, as David did, "It is good for me that I have been afflicted." The Lord hath showed me the vanity of these outward things. That they are the vanity of vanities, and vexation of spirit, that they are but a shadow, a blast, a bubble, and things of no continuance. That we must rely on God Himself, and our whole dependance must be upon Him. If trouble from smaller matters begin to arise in me, I have something at hand to check myself with, and say, why am I troubled? It was but the other day that if I had had the world, I would have given it for my freedom, or to have been a servant to a Christian. I have learned to look beyond present and smaller troubles, and to be quieted under them. As Moses said, "Stand still and see the salvation of the Lord" (Exodus 14.13).

Finis.

Also from Benediction Books ...
Wandering Between Two Worlds: Essays on Faith and Art
Anita Mathias
Benediction Books, 2007
152 pages
ISBN: 0955373700

Available from www.amazon.com, www.amazon.co.uk

In these wide-ranging lyrical essays, Anita Mathias writes, in lush, lovely prose, of her naughty Catholic childhood in Jamshedpur, India; her large, eccentric family in Mangalore, a sea-coast town converted by the Portuguese in the sixteenth century; her rebellion and atheism as a teenager in her Himalayan boarding school, run by German missionary nuns, St. Mary's Convent, Nainital; and her abrupt religious conversion after which she entered Mother Teresa's convent in Calcutta as a novice. Later rich, elegant essays explore the dualities of her life as a writer, mother, and Christian in the United States-- Domesticity and Art, Writing and Prayer, and the experience of being "an alien and stranger" as an immigrant in America, sensing the need for roots.

About the Author

Anita Mathias is the author of *Wandering Between Two Worlds: Essays on Faith and Art.* She has a B.A. and M.A. in English from Somerville College, Oxford University, and an M.A. in Creative Writing from the Ohio State University, USA. Anita won a National Endowment of the Arts fellowship in Creative Nonfiction in 1997. She lives in Oxford, England with her husband, Roy, and her daughters, Zoe and Irene.

Visit Anita's website
http://www.anitamathias.com,
and Anita's blog
http://dreamingbeneaththespires.blogspot.com, (Dreaming Beneath the Spires).

The Church That Had Too Much
Anita Mathias
Benediction Books, 2010
52 pages
ISBN: 9781849026567

Available from www.amazon.com, www.amazon.co.uk

The Church That Had Too Much was very well-intentioned. She wanted to love God, she wanted to love people, but she was both hampered by her muchness and the abundance of her possessions, and beset by ambition, power struggles and snobbery. Read about the surprising way The Church That Had Too Much began to resolve her problems in this deceptively simple and enchanting fable.

About the Author

Anita Mathias is the author of *Wandering Between Two Worlds: Essays on Faith and Art.* She has a B.A. and M.A. in English from Somerville College, Oxford University, and an M.A. in Creative Writing from the Ohio State University, USA. Anita won a National Endowment of the Arts fellowship in Creative Nonfiction in 1997. She lives in Oxford, England with her husband, Roy, and her daughters, Zoe and Irene.

Visit Anita's website
   http://www.anitamathias.com,
and Anita's blog
   http://dreamingbeneaththespires.blogspot.com (Dreaming Beneath the Spires).

www.ingramcontent.com/pod-product-compliance
Lightning Source LLC
Chambersburg PA
CBHW020312150626
46552CB00022B/2817